True Crime Mysterious Cases

A collection of Suspense and Thriller Stories to read

KIMBERLY WEBB

ISBN: 9798690181659

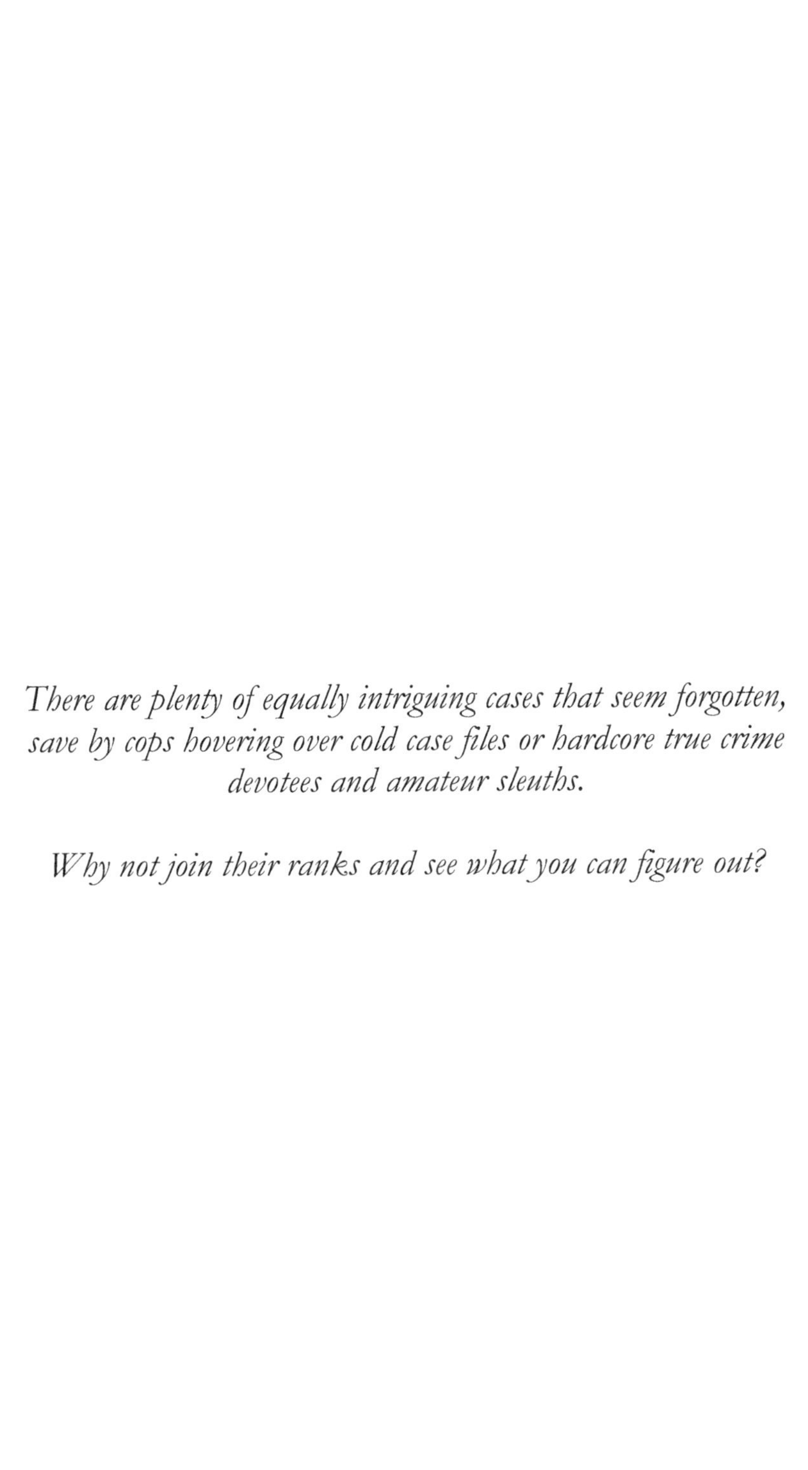

There are plenty of equally intriguing cases that seem forgotten, save by cops hovering over cold case files or hardcore true crime devotees and amateur sleuths.

Why not join their ranks and see what you can figure out?

CONTENTS

TRUE CRIME MYSTERIOUS CASES

1 ELISA LAM AND THE CECIL HOTEL

Case details

21-year-old Canadian resident Elisa Lam was traveling in the United States when she landed in Los Angeles, California on January 29, 2013. Before arriving in LA, Elisa was visiting San Diego. At LA, she stayed at the 600-room Cecil Hotel in downtown near Skidlow. Built in 1927 for business travelers, the hotel was mostly temporary since the 1950s.

Cecil Hotel was once visited by serial murderer Richard Ramirez (also known as Night Stalker) and Austrian Jack Unterweeger who preyed on a prostitute.

The last known sighting of Elisa Lam alive occurred on January 31, 2013. A hotel elevator surveillance video showed that she was behaving strangely in the elevator, talking to someone or me. She is also seen pressing the elevator button twice. Her strange behavior has caused many theories about this case. Some say she has a spiritual episode. Others think she's talking to someone like me. Second, there is a paranormal community that believes ghosts are involved.

After walking away from the elevator, Elisa vanished into a thin air.

Almost three weeks later, on February 19, her naked body was discovered by a maintenance worker in a water tank at the hotel after a hotel guest complained about delicious water and weak water pressure. Her clothes were at the bottom beside her.

The tank is one of four 8-foot-high, 4-foot-diameter tanks with the opening unlocked at the top. The door to the roof is usually locked and the roof itself is protected by an alarm system.

Necropsy and toxicity studies were performed to determine the cause of death. Initially, her death was inconclusive. However, in June 2013, the coroner officially ruled her death due to drowning and bipolar disorder was listed as an important condition. LE saw a sick blog post from Elisa. There were no signs of trauma on the body and there were no drugs or alcohol in her system.

LAPD believes Elisa is bipolar and depressed, and her mental health may have changed due to her own mental health. According to the department, Elisa fell into a water tank and could not go out and be drowned in an accident.

Suicide, murder, strange coincidence
Many have read that Cecil Hotel believes he is suffering from the suicides and murders that happened here.

In 1962, Pauline Otton, 27, jumped to her death through a window on the ninth floor after discussing with her husband. She landed on a sidewalk 90 feet below a pedestrian named George Jainni, 65, and killed him immediately. She was just one of many guests who ended their lives during their stay at the hotel.

"Pigeon Goldie" Osgood, who enjoyed feeding pigeons in a nearby plaza in an unsolved murder case in 1964, was found dead in her room. She was stabbed, strangled, and raped-her room was robbed.

Oddly enough, by the time Eliza stayed in Cecil, the outbreak of tuberculosis was widespread in Skidrow in downtown Los Angeles. The test used to diagnose tuberculosis was called LAM-ELISA, especially in patients with advanced immunosuppression. strange.

Elisa's death is eerily similar to the 2005 movie Dark Water, a remake of the 2002 Japanese movie of the same name, which tells the story of a young woman drowning in a hotel aquarium. A scene in the movie describes an elevator breakdown, and the hero's daughter is named Cecilia.

Is it Elizaram in the elevator?
Some people don't think it's an elevator Eliza. And when I first compare the pictures, I must say I thought the same easily. The picture below is taken from the case's Websleuths thread. I agree that there are some differences between the rightmost photo and the first two photos. So you have to ask: If it's not her, who is it? And where is Elisa?

As if this case wouldn't be strange, we have this: Someone posted on her blog from the time she died until December 2013. .. Funny. hell?

Remaining questions

Many questions remain about Eliza's death and the circumstances surrounding it.

Why did she travel alone?

Why did you decide to stay at Cecil Hotel, a short distance from Skid Row?

Who is she talking to in the video? Or is she talking to her?

Why did she press the buttons on all the elevators?

Did she have a psychotic episode?

How did she get to the aquarium? The roof of the hotel was protected by an alarm system. Had someone gone there without the hotel staff knowing it would have disappeared. Why didn't it disappear?

Did she go on the roof on her own, or did someone push her up there?

Did she access the roof using Fire Escape?

What do you think? Was Elisa's death an accident, a suicide or a murder?

2 MOLLY MARIE YOUNG: MURDER OR SUICIDE?

On March 24, 2012, 21-year-old Molly Mary Young was found shot dead in her former boyfriend's apartment in Block 500, Northwest Ridge Drive, Carbondale, IL. Ritchie Minton, who was terribly drunk, called Molly around 3:00 am and claimed that she needed help. Molly didn't drink herself.

Shortly after Molly arrived at the apartment, she was shot in the head. The .45 semi-automatic 1911 handgun used to kill was by chance owned by Minton himself.

The 911 call was made by Minton's roommate Wesley Romack at 9:02 am, several hours after Molly's death.

For some reason, Carbondale PD handed over the investigation to the Illinois State Police, who arrived shortly after calling 911.

Molly's hands had no powder residue and the gun had no fingerprints. This means it was not suicide. A police report released after her death showed that investigators carried out a bullet-residue test with the hands of Molly, Ritchie, and Wesley. The results were negative for all three.

So what is the kicker in this case? Well, Minton has never

committed a crime. And neither of his roommates.

Why are you listening After all, Minton is a former telecommunicator for Carbondale Police. He was hired there at the time of filming. He is also the son of Franklin County Sheriff's deputy for many years. Minton has already defended by the time Illinois police arrived that morning for the investigation. Seven, Count' Those, SEVEN individuals came to an independent investigator, saying the CPD was on the scene much earlier than when the 911 call was made. Some people believe this is a huge police   cover-up.

Molly's death was not considered a suicide or murder after the shooting. It was considered "suspicious" because there was insufficient evidence of murder or suicide.

Minton claimed there were two 6-inch long scars under his face and under his arms, which must have occurred during a CPR attempt against Molly.

During a coroner's investigation, Molly was found to be depressed and threatening suicide with text messages to both Minton and Romack. Dark journal entries were also listed, but some were more than two years old.

In August 2013, Mike County, a Jackson County attorney, announced that the suit had been closed and the suit was closed.

On June 30, 2014, Molly's father, Larry, filed an unlawful death suit against Ritchie Minton.

3 WHO WAS THE DOODLER?

Well, this is a serial killer I've never heard of. People who know their identity remain a mystery to the general public, but not to the police.

Between January 1974 and September 1975, there were six murders and three assaults in the San Francisco gay community. In the attack, the murderer met other men at gay clubs and restaurants outside San Francisco. He is usually named "The Doodler" (also known as "The Black Doodler") because he sketched men before they had sex and then stabbed them. The police believe they committed the murder after being shamed by the homosexual experience.

From 1976 to 1977, police interrogated certain young people about murder and attacks. In fact, he was identified by two survivors, but no arrests were made. Mainly because survivors do not want to go out. One was a famous entertainer and the other was a diplomat. It didn't look like it was out of the closet in the 70s. People lost it, lost their jobs, and were basically abandoned in society.

The suspect spoke freely to the police, who had never publicly disclosed his name.

Herbery Milk, who advocated for gay rights at this time (Shaun

Penn played him in the movie "Milk") said, "I don't want them exposed. I can understand their position. We respect the pressure society has placed on them."

Okay, Harvey, whatever. But now it's 2012 and the world is in a different place than it was in the late '70s. Why don't the survivors come forward? I'm sure they are out of the closet now. And more importantly, why didn't the police reveal the suspect's name?

You may have found some victim names.

Gerald Cavaneau, 50 years old. His body was discovered on January 27, 1974, at 1:30 am on the beach near Boulevard Uroa.

Stig Berlin, 40 years old. His body was found on February 19, 1974 at 1:45 pm in an apartment on Hyde Street.

His body was found on a beach near Lincoln Way on July 7, 1974. He was stabbed and died.

In 1978, five more gay murders occurred in San Mateo County in a manner similar to the Doodler murder, wondering if police were connected. It is unknown if there was a connection.

The fact that Doodler sketched the victim before the attack may mean that he was a local artist. If so, it could suggest that he, like the trophy, loved to have something that remembers the victim.

It is worth noting here that San Francisco PDs also dealt with the Zodiac Killer and Zebra murders during the Doodler killing. The zodiac killer remains unknown, but was arrested for killing Zebra. Needless to say, SFPD was completely raising his hand.

But why not announce the suspect's name after all these years? Why is there such little information about this case?

4 WHO KILLED CHRISTINE JESSOP?

On October 3, 1984, nine-year-old Christine Jessop got off the school bus at around 3:50 pm in Queensville, Ontario, Canada. The house was empty Her father, Robert, recently began to be sentenced to 18 months for mishandling funds at a detention center in Toronto, and her mother, Janet, worked with Christine's brother, Kenneth (14). It was a.

Between 4 and 4:30 pm, Christine was seen walking to a nearby grocery store to buy bubble gum. This was the last sighting of Christine alive.

Shortly thereafter, Janet and Kenneth arrived home. Christine's book bag was sitting at the kitchen counter, but no girl was anywhere. Her parents called a friend and began looking for a neighborhood, including a nearby park. nothing.

Between 7 and 8 Janet called the police. Soon, the York Provincial Police began a large-scale search for the girl, but all attempts to find Christine failed.

Christine's birthday (November 29th) came in and out without Christine that year. Then on December 31, almost three months after his disappearance, her body was found in the woods, about 30 miles from his Queensville home. She was raped and stabbed many times. Semen was found in her panties, but in 1984 there was no way to identify the source of semen. The arrival of DNA tests did not arrive until 1985. However, the panties were kept in evidence lockers for the time being.

Shortly after Christine disappeared, police approached Christine's neighbor Guy Paul Morin (23). They felt he would fit the profile of Christine's murderer who would have been in his mid-twenties at the time of the killing. Morin was a little lonely living with his mother and father and working at a local furniture store, Interior International Limited. Oddly enough, Morin had no criminal record before the murder.

Technicians at the Ontario Center for Forensics testified that the red fiber found in Morin's car came from the sweater Kristin wore on his fateful day. The prosecution claimed this linked Morin as Kristin. In addition, two prison snitches. X" testified that Morin confessed to killing Christine.

The way juries consider these snitches to be trustworthy is beyond me. It's very easy to lie down. It's also very easy to say that someone said something to you, whether it was true or false. What I want to know is whether these two snitches get something by testifying the prosecution.

After two trials, acquitted in the first trial, Guy Paul Morin was convicted of Christine's rape and murder on July 23, 1992 and sentenced to death in prison.

That should have been it, right?

Well usually. There was only one minor problem.

A 1995 DNA test showed that Morin's DNA was inconsistent with that found in Christine's panties. After a protest based on the DNA report, Morin was released and eventually awarded nearly $1.5 million.

So who killed Christine Jessop?

Well, it remains a mystery and the case is unsolved.

In June 1992, Christine's brother Ken testified at Morin's trial that he and two friends (a pair of brothers) had sex with Kristin many times from the age of two to two years before the murder. .. He was 7 years old when he started and his brothers were 9 and 11 years old.

The police officer ruled him out, probably because of his DNA.

But is it possible that one of his friends committed a crime? Before this disappearance and murder, what was the chance that the girl who was raped (says a 9-year-old girl was raped because she did not consent to sexual activity) wasn't killed by one of the rapists?

Moment of opportunity for another freak? Yes, it is possible, but is it possible in this particular case? I'm not sure.

Police officers immediately pointed to Morin and there was no physical evidence to guide them. I'm convinced that the public pressure to catch the maniac was related to it. After the killing of Christine, there was a huge public protest against justice.

The fact that Christine's murderer is still large remains. Has he killed since 1984?

Also, are there any Christine incidents related to other young girls killed in the area at the same time? Also nine Sharin Morningstar Keenan were abducted in January 1983. Her body was discovered the following February. Allison Parrot disappeared at the age of 11 in July 1986. Nicole Morin, 8 years old, disappeared from Etobicoke in Toronto, Ontario in 1985. She remains missing to date.

5 WHO KILLED THESE MONTANA WOMEN OVER A DECADE AGO?

In 1998 and 2000, two women were brutally killed in Montana. To date, the case remains open.

On Sunday, November 15, 1998, Miranda Fenner was working at The Movie Store on 419 Main Street in Laurel, Montana when an unknown raider came in and took her to the back of the store. , I stabbed my neck many times. The perpetrator also cut her throat and fled the scene. Miranda managed to crawl out of the front door when the passing driver found her and called the police. She was taken to a hospital where she was sentenced to death. They believe she was stabbed from 7:45 pm to 8:15 pm

The murderer left no evidence and did not steal anything from the store or Miranda himself. At the time, Miranda was the only one working in the store.

34-year-old Jeannette "Charlie" Atwater
Early in the morning of January 16, 2000, a burning car was discovered in Billings, Montana with its body in the trunk. The body was identified as Jeannette "Charlie" Atwater, a divorced mother with three small children.

Autopsy revealed no other signs of fatal injury, such as bullet wounds or head trauma, and she did not appear to be gagged or tied up. .. They also don't mention how or where she was placed in the trunk.

Prior to the killing, Charlie was at a local bar on 231 Main Street (now Hotel) with a colleague from the Napa Distribution Center. The last time she saw it was around 2 am when the bar announced the closing time. No one saw Charlie leaving the bar or going to the car. A bar worker said he had no hassles at the parking lot that night.

The detective confirmed footage from the surveillance cameras in the bar, but Charlie was not found in the crowd. Her colleague said she did not leave with their group.

By 2:15am, the car park was empty.

The Senex gas station opposite the bar is still there today. An unidentified man paid $ 1 worth of gas after 3am. The footage shows a Caucasian man in his thirties, about 5 feet tall and 10 inches tall. His face had brown acne scars and was wearing a warm-up or jogging suit on his pants and jacket. The clerk later said that the men were wearing expensive, or at least strong, aftershaves or colognes. The clerk only described the car as a small brown hatchback with orange stripes. It was unknown whether the man had put gas in the car or container, and the clerk did not know if the man was alone.

6 THE SHORT FAMILY MURDER

On August 15, 2002, the bodies of Michael and Mary Short were discovered at their home in Henry County, Virginia. Both were hit by the head and the telephone line was cut before the killing.

Michael was found on an enclosed carport sofa. Mary was in the bedroom. Their 9-year-old daughter Jennifer is missing and police believe she was taken from an unmade bed.

Authorities initially suspected the girl escaped and escaped during the shooting (Associated Press, 2002).

The motive was not robbery. There was $485 cash left at the kitchen counter.

A large-scale search for the girl and the murderer continued.

Finally, on September 25, 2002, Jennifer's body was discovered near the riverbed in North Carolina. She was also shot in the head.

The suspect appeared immediately. His name was Gary Bowman. Jennifer's body was found near a trailer owned by Bowman. The day after Michael's and Mary's body was discovered, he fled to Canada, but was taken back and had a violent interview with authorities. In 2007 he was excluded as a suspect.

In 2018, police released for new assistance.

To date, the murderer has not been arrested and the case remains unresolved.

* Updated August 24, 2019

True Crime Diva Thoughts
This case reminds me a little of the Joseph Duncan case. In May 2005 he killed three. Brenda Gruene, her boyfriend Mark McKenzie, and her 13-year-old son Slade Gruene (home in Coeur d'Alene, Idaho). Her two youngest children, Dylan (9) and Shasta (8), were kidnapped by Duncan. Dylan was later killed by Duncan, but Shasta survived and was found in a Denny's restaurant with the abductee. Both children were repeatedly molested by Duncan. Duncan was detained by police but confessed in 1997 that he had killed 14-year-old Anthony Martinez and 11-year-old Samiejo White (11) and his sister Carmen Cubias (9) in Beaumont, California. Pan handle in Seattle, Washington. Duncan was sentenced to imprisonment.

I remember reading that Duncan had abducted Dylan and Shasta by killing Brenda Gruene, her boyfriend, Mark, and his son Slade.

I wonder what happened at Jennifer Short. Maybe her parents were killed, so the killer could reach Jennifer. She was not killed at home. She was taken to another place and killed. why?

The area where the shorts lived is small and rural. So is the place where Jennifer's body was found. So this wonders if the murderer was known to the victim and was at home.

When I was investigating this case, I came across a serial killer Gary Hilton. He was convicted in 2008 of killing Meredith Emerson. He was subsequently associated with the 2007 killing of an old couple in North Carolina and a woman in Florida. Hilton resembles a composite of suspects in a short-term murder case

His eyes attract me. The photo below is a 1995 mugshot seven years before the short murder. His face and eye shape resemble a sketched man.

When I saw the Hilton, I also thought about the kidnapper of Mikaela Galecht. However, it was explained that her kidnapper was in her 20s in 1988. Hilton would have been 42 years old. She said the man had a "fox's eye."

Hilton didn't seem to like age, so I think he could have kidnapped Michaela if we could connect him to California. He was a castaway, so he probably left for a while in California in 1988.

I really hope that someday the short family will have justice. They didn't deserve what happened to them. I would like to think that the killer is mentally distressed by what he did, but it is very doubtful that he even cares.

7 THE STRANGE DEATH OF COLONEL PHILIP SHUE

On April 16, 2003, Colonel Philippe Shoe, 54, left Texas to work. Two hours later he was found dead in the car. It looks like the victim of a car accident. The car collapsed to the driver's side, resulting in severe head injury to Philip. He was immediately killed.

This case was immediately strange. When police officials appeared on the scene, they discovered more than they had negotiated.

Philip was tired and had a tear on his T-shirt. There they could see a 6-inch vertical gouache on his chest. At the top of the 6-inch gouache entrance, there are at least 5 scratch marks, which the autopsy report matches with the hesitant mark. Both of his nipples were surgically removed accurately. The fifth finger of the left hand was amputated, and the left ear had torn to the bone. Duct tape was hanging on both his wrist and the top of the boots.

What was the first decision in this strange case? suicide.

Dr Vincent Di Mayo's autopsy led to the discovery. He said there were traces of lidocaine (anesthetic) in his system, indicating that Philip had injected himself to avoid the pain of the amputation. He would have injected it in the middle of each nipple and chest.

According to world-renowned pathologist Dr. Cyril Wecht, the problem with the suicide sentence (one of many) is that 1) no injection marks were found on his body, 2) the level of lidocaine It wasn't high enough to relieve the pain. , Examined the autopsy report at the request of Philip's wife Tracy.

So who wanted to kill Philip if it was a murder?

Well, it turns out that Philip's ex-wife Nancy Shu had him a $1 million life insurance policy. And you know how some people get for money – they kill for it.

Apparently, as part of Philip's and Nancy's settlement of the divorce in 1992, she received the right to own his life insurance policy. From the late 1990s, Philip requested Nancy to cancel, but of course refused. He also went to the insurance company where the insurance contract was written and told them he was afraid of his life. But they told him he couldn't revoke the policy because Nancy was the owner. They remained valid.

Interestingly, Nancy was a certified sex therapist who had studied sadomasochism practices.

Here's what Tracy had to say about this during an interview with Troy Roberts in the "48-Hour Mystery":

"Do you think your husband was tortured by someone who is familiar with sadomasochistic techniques?" Roberts asks.

"I think the injuries he suffered are in line with the acts of sadism, and they are certainly sexual in nature," Tracy replies.

"Forgive" Roberts continues, "But I have to ask this question. Was your husband interested in this fetish himself?"

"No he didn't," says Tracy. "And it's interesting that you ask that question. You've been asking that question because you're actually the first person in a five-year time frame, and that's the right question to ask. I think."

She refused when Nancy was asked to undergo a polygraph test.

Two months after Philip's death, Tracy sued Nancy and the insurance companies, USAA and Northwestern Mutual, in an attempt to prevent Nancy from recovering her claims. Tracy argued that the insurance company had been warned about the threat to Philip's life and had a legal obligation to cancel police, but they did not.

Tracy's lawyer demanded that Nancy answer their questions in a deposit, but she begged Fifth, which she would do twenty more times.

Does this sound like an innocent woman to you?

Tracy believes her husband was abducted, tortured, and killed, and believes Nancy was somehow involved.

Before he died, he received an anonymous letter to "be careful." This man was worried that something very bad would happen to him.

And it happened.

Apparently, this letter had no meaning to law enforcement or military authorities.

Two years after Philip's death, the military issued a 20-page report called Psychoanatomy. It concluded that Philip was depressed, paranoid and suicidal.

However, Dr. Douglas Dionne, Philip's own psychiatrist, said he was responsive to treatment and did not believe that his patient committed suicide. Dionne said six months before his death, he had an uneasy dream that his car would go out of control on the way to work and that violence would hit him.

Roger Anderson, chief investigator of the case, never believed that Philip's death was a suicide, and today he fully supports Tracy in her efforts to bring justice to her husband.

After many years of fighting to kill Philip's death, Judge Bill Palmer changed his decision from suicide to murder in an insurance suit in 2008, five years after Philip's death.

To date no one has been arrested for his killing.

8 THE ABDUCTION AND MURDER OF TAMMY ZYWICKI

In August 1992, Tamiji Wiki disappeared due to a car breakdown at the I-80 in Illinois. Her body was found a week later in Missouri, but no arrests have been made so far.

About Tammy Zywicki

Tammy Jo Zywicki was born on 13 March 1971 in Pleasant Hill, Pennsylvania, to Henry and Joanji Wiki. She was their only daughter of three children.

During the six months of 1992, Tammy toured Italy, Portugal and Spain to study in Madrid. In August of that year, she was to begin her senior year at Grinnell University in Grinnell, Iowa. So she majored in Art History and Spanish and worked in the Sports Information Department of the Sports Secretariat. She was also a member of the college football team. Tammy is expected to graduate in May 1993 and she was planning to become a sports photographer.

Tammy was trying to start her internship at the Art Institute of Chicago on September 8th, which lasted until December, but had no chance.

About the case

In August 1992, 21-year-old Tammy Wicky and her younger brother, 19-year-old Darren, left Pittsburgh, PA for the Midwest to attend college. Along the way, the two managed to repair the Indiana's overheated engine. Darren put some oil in it and the car was fine at that time. The two arrived in Evanston, Illinois on Saturday, August 22nd. Tammy stayed in Evanston and departed for Grinnell College around 1:00 pm the next day. The drive would have taken her about 4-5 hours.

A few hours later, around 5 pm, a trooper in Illinois found Tammy's white 1985 Pontiac T1000, about two miles east of Utica along Interstate 80, and issued it as abandoned. The hood was down, the doors were locked, the keys were gone, and there were no signs of cheating. Her clothes and camera were still in the car.

When Tammy couldn't call his mother Joan in advance, Joanne called the Illinois police to let her know that she had arrived at Grinnell safely.

Search of Tammy Zywicki
Tammy finally wore a white shirt, green shorts, white socks and gray running shoes. Her mother probably said that her hair was ponytail (Lenhart, 1992).

The Illinois State Guard brought a helicopter to aerial scan the cornfield along the I-80. They found nothing.

A state police dog unit was brought in and friends and family handed out missing posters.

In Iowa, 16 college friends promised to card the highway 24 hours a day. They fan out east and west of the Interstate and are ready to distribute 2,500 flyers. (Renhart).

Trucker helped deliver some posters to some states, as did other college students across the United States

Despite a massive search, Tammy didn't see anywhere.

Discovery and investigation

Witnesses saw Tammy getting out of the car, opening the hood, and standing by the road at about 3:20 pm. Other witnesses claimed to have seen a man helping Tammy by car between 3:20 and 16:00 pm. A male tractor trailer was parked near Tammy's Pontiac. The trucker was a white man in his thirties or forties and was described as over six feet tall and had dark hair with a collar length. He was driving a 5-axle semi-trailer with a brown diagonal stripe across the cab and trailer on a white background.

A week later, around 11:00 am on September 1, a female body was found along I-44 in Missouri, 33 miles east of the Oklahoma border. The victim was wearing a T-shirt that read "East Side Eagles Soccer 1989." Tammy graduated from Eastside High School in Greenville, South Carolina in 1989. The victim was first wrapped in a white sheet, then a dark red blanket, and duct tape tied at both ends. According to one source, the victim's hair was reddish brown rather than blonde. She was sexually assaulted and stabbed seven times – six wounds on her chest and one on her arm.

Later, Tammy's items, such as a music wristwatch with an umbrella, were discovered and lost.

The FBI Task Force was assigned to this case. Fourteen investigators tried to gather all the information about Tammy's murderer.

Des Moines truck driver Robert Barrington, 24, went to the police. He said he was chatting with Jerry on his CB radio. The two met and decided to have a coffee together. Both men stopped looking at the driver stuck at the I-80 in Illinois. Robert told police that he saw a young blonde woman climb a man's gray Chevrolet celebrity with a Nebraska plate at 1 am on August 24. Robert headed to his destination in Utah.

Then came a promising lead.

Ronnie Beer Blot

An unnamed female witness called MTF. She told them she was driving on an I-80 and saw Tammy standing behind her car. A green pickup truck was parked, the front of which was facing the front of Tammy's car. A man stood next to the truck and looked like he was helping a student. The nurse later recognized a man named Ronnie Biablot when he came to her office with his wife who was doing a blood test after learning about Tammy's disappearance. (Colimore, 2005).

Beerblot's wife, Carey, was wearing a musical watch similar to what Tammy wore before Tammy's disappearance and pointed it out to the nurse. Carey said Viablot gave her it.

The watch had an umbrella on its face and played the song "Raindrops Keep Falling on My Head". This watch was consistent with the missing watch description she had on Tammy's disappearance, but was not recovered after the body was discovered.

Carrie later denied that Biablot handed her a watch, but admitted to the police that she could not offer him an alibi.

When police led and tracked, they learned that the Beerbot had driven a green pickup like the eyewitnesses saw on the I-80. He had previously lived near where Tammy was last seen and was visiting relatives at that time. In addition, he lived in Missouri within 30 miles of where Tammy's body was found.

Biabrot also had a criminal record and was considered a "violent felony." He was sentenced to two years of imprisonment for two years due to violence by armed forces, attempted murder, and was released on parole in 1990, when he started driving a truck. The cicada he was driving in August 1992 was Kenmore. Tammy's body, a red blanket with the Kenworth logo, was wrapped.

He had no alibi when police interviewed Biabrot. POlice took blood and hair samples but couldn't run the test due to lack of DNA recovered from Tammy's body.

Biabrot was never arrested. He died on June 17, 2002, at the age of 41.

Another suspect

Bruce Mendenhall was a trucker convicted in 2007 of the murder of prostitute 25-year-old Sarah Halbert. He later admitted more killings. Mendenhall would have been about 40 at the time of Tammy's killing. But most of his victims were the prostitutes he picked up at the truck stops he frequented. Born from a good family, Tammy was an athletic and student, not a prostitute.

Unfortunately, Biabot died in 2002 at the age of 41. So even if he kills Tammy, we never know. To my knowledge, Mendenhall is still breathing.

To date, I'm thinking about her, that's why I wrote this post. Someday, you'll definitely know who killed her. Even if we don't, I continue to be convinced it was Ronnie Beerbott.

9 THE UNSOLVED MURDER OF HEAVEN LASHAE ROSS

On August 19, 2003, 11-year-old Heaven LaShae Ross left the Willowbrook Trailer Park Northport Trailer, Alabama, and walked 50 yards to the school bus stop on Hunter Creek Road, where it disappeared into a thin sky.

At 7am, Heaven with the nickname Shea left the house and headed for the bus stop. Her 13-year-old sister Alex left five minutes ago. The bus will arrive at the stop around 7:25 am.

After the thunder, Shay's stepfather, 33-year-old Kevin Thompson, took the girl to school by car to a bus stop. He left home at 7:1 am, one minute after Shay left. Only Shay's sister was waiting when he arrived.

I reported seeing my neighbor pass by her, but another neighbor wasn't down two trailers. This means Shay disappeared between these two trailers.

Thompson returned to their trailer house and called the police.

A large search started, but it didn't help.

Three years later, in December 2006, the body was found in an abandoned house along a dirt road in the countryside of Holt, a Tuscaloosa community about eight miles from Shae's home.

Evidence suggests that the body was from Heavenly Lasheiros.

To date, no one has been arrested for her killing, and her death was undecided.

Police probably thought that Shay's killing was related to Shannon Paulk's killing and Teresa Dean's abduction. All three girls were 11 years old and were kidnapped within a few days (separate years) of each other in August and lived in a trailer park. Shannon disappeared on August 16, 2001, and Teresa disappeared on August 15, 1999.

However, after Shay's body was discovered, authorities did not believe the case was related.

Five weeks after Shae went missing, a fire broke out in her house. It was limited to one side of her bedroom. The marshal decided that the fire was suspicious.

No one has ever been arrested for the killing of Shae, and the case remains unresolved.

10 THE MYSTERIOUS MURDER OF SEVEN-YEAR-OLD DALTON MESARCHIK

Dalton Alexander Mesarchik was born on April 29, 1995 in George E. Scott and Michelle Messarik.

In the spring of 2003, Dalton was a freshman at Centennial School in Streator, Illinois. The town is a small town that spans two counties, La Salle and Livingstone. Dalton lived in La Salle County.

Dalton loved Harley-Davidson motorcycles, collected Harley-Davidson souvenirs, riding bicycles, art, and school.

He dreamed of owning his Harley one day. Unfortunately that was not the case.

Case details
On March 26, 2003, seven-year-old Dalton Mesarkic in Streeter, Illinois disappeared from his home at 400 blocks on Morel Street. ..

Dalton was not a regular church or youth program regular. He has been there only a few times since August 2002.

Early reports said Dalton was waiting at the front porch at around 7:15 pm for a church van to pick up.

The church van never showed and Dalton disappeared. His parents called the church only to find out that the program was canceled, but no one in the church called them.

It was later revealed that the van driver was unable to drive the car as he visited a sick relative outside the state. Usually, churches usually call when vans can't pick up their children and allow parents to take their children to church. Obviously it wasn't here.

Dalton's mother, Michelle, reported that he was missing at police at 8:34 pm

Police brought Bloodhound to the scene the next morning. The dog traced Dalton's scent from the pouch to the middle of the street. So the investigators believed that he got into the car or was forced. They thought at that time that the one who had abducted Dalton might have been driving a van similar to a church van.

500 volunteers gathered at the City Hall to start looking for Dalton. Joined the investigation were Illinois State Police, FBI, La Salle and Livingston County Sheriff's Office.

State Police Sergeant Bill Heinrich organized the group into a team of 10 and fanned out across the entire Streeter area. Boats and horses were brought in as part of the search (Stanmar, 2003).

Found dalton
The search was canceled at approximately 11:33 am on Thursday, March 27, 2003. Fishermen found a fully dressed corpse of Dalton floating on the Vermilion River near the Vermilion Boat Club, two miles south of the Streeter in Livingston County.

It was then revealed that Dalton had been beaten dead by a small £3 bench-top professional hammer sold only at Kmart. The blood on the handle matched that of Dalton. In some reports his limbs were restrained, but police did not confirm this.

Thirty investigators in Streator, Lassalle, Livingston, FBI and state police were focused on tracking nearly 70 leads (Stanmar and Guetersioh, 2003).

Police interviewed Dalton Mesarchik's friends and family and local sex offenders. For unknown reasons, Dalton's parents were excluded as suspects. According to a report in 2015, it passed the polygraph test.

Investigators surveyed the neighborhood and made roadside confirmations.

Search and rescue teams of the Natural Resources Police Department and the Pontiac Fire Department worked for several hours to search the river where Dalton's body was found (Stanmar and Getersio). Police said they were searching the river for forensic evidence.

Despite extensive research, no Dalton Mesarchic murderers have been found. To date, he has never been arrested for the killing of Dalton and no suspect has been appointed. Police had an unknown suspect shortly after the murder, which was another dead end.

Dalton Mesarchik's funeral
Dalton Mesarchik took a rest on Tuesday, April 1, 2003.

When the mourner left Elias Funeral Center towards Hillcrest Memorial Park, a boy known by local motorcyclists as a "Little Dude" was Harley-Davidson Bikes (Wieczorkiewicz, 2003), a favorite of children in the world. In honor of, he was given a funeral procession for a biker.

The rumored factory has been working hard since the killing of Dalton. One of the big rumors is Dalton's own sister, Deana Mesarchik, who killed him. In 2015, 25-year-old Deana attended a cable talk show and passed the lie detector test. Michel Mesarchik said he wants to squash the rumors that Diana is involved.

Passion Crime
Rumors aside, I have to question whether Dalton Mesarchik knew of the murderer. Why didn't he scream when he was

abducted? Perhaps the murderer was driving a van and thought it was a church van, like the police guessed in 2003.

This murder was malicious. In other words, how cold do you have to be to kill a 7 year old child and die? How angry are you This is a crime of passion and I think Dalton knew his hitman.

There is no mention of whether Dalton was sexually assaulted. I don't know why the police didn't mention it. If he was, it is a motive and it is likely that a sex offender killed him. If not, it was probably someone he knew in my opinion.

Anyone who knows where the murder of Dalton, the hammer used to kill it, or where the body of Dalton was found can contact the following contacts: Located at daltonm@isp.state.il.us.

32

11 THE MYSTERIOUS MURDER OF DYKE AND KAREN RHOADS

Paris, Illinois is a small rural village in Edgar County in the eastern part of the state. For the most part, once bragging about as "the most secretive in the Midwest," it's a quiet town. Few would think that a town of this size has a deadly secret. But yes. The town is known for honeymoon murders and many other unsolved murders, and even the Sicilian mafia.

On March 22, 1986, Dyke and Cullen Road were married at the Lake Ridge Christian Church in Paris, Illinois. Dyke was 27 years old and worked for Chemloan in Terre Haute, Indiana. Karen, 25, worked at the Morgan manufacturing plant in Paris owned by Robert Morgan.

The couple moved to a two-story house at 433 E. Court Street in Paris. They were madly in love and were looking forward to spending the rest of their lives together.

Unfortunately for them, it never happened.

Deadly fire
Terry Newman, who lives in Paris, lived near his house in Rhodes. Around 6 am on July 6, 1986, Terry woke up to the sound of breaking glass. He looked out the window and saw Roaz's house

in flames.

Terry dressed and ran outside the south side of the burning house. He tried to open the side door, but it was locked. Then he started knocking on the door trying to get the couple up. When that didn't work, he ran around to the front door and found that it was locked as well, but he started pounding on it anyway. Terry yelled at the top of his lungs, alerting Dyke and Karen, but his efforts failed.

A female neighbor contacted the fire department at 4:39 am. They soon arrived at the scene. When the firefighters were able to enter the house, they discovered that Dyke and Karen Road's naked bodies were lying on the floor of the master bedroom on the second floor. It was obvious that the two were killed because blood was flowing throughout the bedroom.

The fire started behind the house with little damage to the front and the second floor (Binder, 1986). The bedroom in which the body was found had little damage from the fire.

autopsy

Edgar County coroner David Dick performed an autopsy at Dyke and Karen Road. Dyke was stabbed 28 times from behind. That is, he was probably asleep when first attacked. Karen suffered 26 stings and had a defensive wound on her hand. She awakens and shows that she fought for her life.

The autopsy report also showed that Dyke had 0.03 percent alcohol in his blood and 0.065 percent alcohol in his urine. No drug was found in his system. No drug or alcohol was found in Karen's system.

McFatridge said the killings were random, but that may not have been the case.

What Karen saw

Karen talked to her sister and one of her brother-in-law about the case at work. One night when the call came in, she was working. A male caller asks his boss, Robert Morgan. Karen told the caller that Morgan had just left the office, but when she looked out the window she saw Morgan still in the parking lot. The caller said to Karen, "This is a very important call. And I really need to talk to him. Run and tell him that "Chicago" is calling? She looked into the trunk of an open car and saw a machine gun. Karen said he said Morgan, "Why are you here? You shouldn't have seen this."

The incident scared Karen, and she told her brother-in-law, James Tate, that she was going to file a notice and quit her job. James later told the FBI that he had told the PD of Paris all this shortly after the killing, but the interview was previously undocumented.

Tim Busby has dated Karen, who had a close relationship with his mother, Marilyn, after they separated. Karen and Marilyn were having lunch at Danville's country club. Karen told Marilyn that an employee at a Morgan manufacturing company named Mark "Smoke" Barba was causing her a lot of trouble, which is getting worse. Karen said he needs to get another job.

Smoke Barba was Robert Morgan's right arm. Investigators never questioned him, even if his name was mentioned several times during the first two months of the investigation.

Even more surprisingly, police interviewed Robert Morgan once only if you could believe it. "Mike McFatridge kept us away from other suspects," investigator Jack Eckerty said a few years later, although Morgan was always a suspect. (2009 Callahan)

Instead, McFatridge focused specifically on the two men and decided to defeat them, even if they had to be costly or lied to get the job done.

Arrest of two innocent men
On January 21, 1987, 41-year-old Parisian Herb Whitlock pleaded guilty to illegal possession of controlled substances. Deputy Sheriff Edgar arrested him on April 5, 1986, allegedly possessing 15.6 grams of cocaine (Monson, 1987).

One month after being pleaded guilty, Paris and Illinois police officers arrested construction worker Gordon Randy Steidol, 35, and charged him and Herb Whitlock with the killing of Dyke and Karen Rhodes. did. For strange reasons, they were not charged with arson at the time.

A grand jury hearing was convened in March 1987, when McFatridge claimed that Herb and Randy had killed Dyke and Karen Lord due to poor drug trafficking.

Mr McFatridge told the jury that on July 6, 1986, two men met at a local bar with plans to pick up a particular woman. He also said through a testimony of 30-year-old Debra Reinbolt that she, Randy, Whitlock, and another passenger, Derrell Herrington, plan to prove that they left the bar and headed to Rhodes' home. .. While there, Reinbolt held Karen Road and Herb and Randy stabbed Dyke with a knife borrowed from Reinbolt. Then Whitlock stabbed Karen and killed him.

Herrington was probably sleeping in the car while the others were at home. Steidol awakens Herrington and takes him to the house of Rhodes. The corpse, showing him, said, "This is what happens to your family when you say something." (Burrows, 1987).

Then, two men broke fire in the kitchen and bedroom with gasoline, McFatridge said.

Reinbolt also claimed that Whitlock told her "... had to take care of Dyke."

Two witnesses
A murder trial is unlikely to find more than two failed, unreliable witnesses than these two.

Drunken town
The drunken town, aka Derrell Herrington, is unbelievable enough to be a witness. Not only was he always wasted from the heart, he was also arrested for two felony charges for his history of deceptive practices and mental health problems.

Herrington alleged that Randy Steidle and Herb Whitlock were murdered because of a worsening drug trade with Dyke. He said he knew this because he was at the scene of the crime when the crime broke out. But Dyke was a pot smoker, and that was where his drug use went.

Also... he never said Debra Reimbolt was there at the time of the murder. At the same time he was there.

Two years after his statement, Herrington withdrew, saying police had provided him with beer and whiskey before the interview.

"That night Gary Wheat and Jack Eccati brought me. Jim Parrish came. They made me drink... beer and wine and whiskey... police station... Jim Parrish. Dwelling... Dwelling where he lives... I was there day and night... They lied to my wife I'm in. They took me to Indianapolis to my wife I said." (Callahan in 2009)

Town drag
Five months after Herrington issued the statement, Debra Reinbolt also appeared. Now, let's say the prosecution didn't know what the word "trustworthy" obviously meant. why?

Debra Reinbolt was an alcoholic drug user. Between 1985 and 1987, she drank one to two cases of beer and smoked a couple of marijuana a day. Moreover, she took two or three lines of amphetamine and cocaine twice a week (Burrows).

So why did she remember something? It was about a year later.

Two trials and two silly convictions
Herb Whitlock's murder trial began in May 1987 on behalf of defense lawyer Ron Turin. The Randy Steidol trial began in June 1987 after the Herb trial, and he was represented by John Muller, a lawyer in Charleston.

As mentioned above, Reinbolt and Herrington testified in both cases and explained what might have occurred on July 6, 1986.

From 48 hours:

"Big confusion. Everything didn't go well, they just frightened Dyke to give it a try, and then get out of hand," Reinbolt says.

Reinbolt argued that he knew Whitlock and Steidl through the use of drugs and saw both stabbed Dyke Rhoads.

When I asked Karen what was going on at that point, she was about to get out of bed and I went there and said everything was fine.

Reinbolt claimed that while Karen was stabbing her, he arrested him and used her husband's knife to kill them.

Reinbolt's story impressed police, especially when she accurately described the broken lamp found in Rhodes' bedroom.

Two juries believed both eyewitness accounts. In 1987, these two men were convicted despite physical evidence linking the men to the killings, an unwavering protest of innocence, and a witness who said they were together on the night of the murder. It was Herb Whitlock was sentenced to imprisonment for the killing of Karen Lord. Steidol received the death penalty for both murders.

In 1999 Steidl and Whitlock finally received the most credible support.

David Protes, a professor of journalism at Northwestern University, and his four students began to re-examine the crime in an attempt to find out who killed the couple.

"It stabbed me from the beginning that this is a likely miscarriage of justice," says Protess. Protes says there was no physical evidence that clearly linked the two men to crime.
"This young couple has been tragically stabbed more than 50 times," he says. "These men would have been covered in blood. There would have been blood in their cars. There would have been blood in their clothes. Someone would have seen them with blood. Hair, There would have been some fiber, something that would connect them to the crime scene. We did nothing." (48 hours)

Finally, Randy Steidl was released in 2004, followed by Herb Whitlock in 2008.

In 2013, Randy Steidle Steidle won his second (first in 2011 against Illinois police) multi-million dollar judgment in his lawsuit against those who surrounded him in prison.

12 THE TRAGIC, UNSOLVED MURDER OF HOGAN'S HEROES STAR BOB CRANE

Born July 13, 1928, Robert "Bob" Crane was a popular Hollywood actor best known for his title role in the popular television show "The Hero of Hogan". After the show was cancelled, Crane eventually moved to the theater and landed on part of the drama "Beginner's Luck", which is being performed in Scottsdale, Arizona. It was there on June 29, 1978, when somebody strangled him in his apartment with an electrical cord before hitting him with a blunt, supposedly camera tripod.

Despite the already notable death of a beloved celebrity, the incident was even brighter after the Crane continued to be a very mean event in his personal life. Attracted attention. He slept with countless women both before and after marriage, and was often proved to have taken lewd encounters and even photographed them. This meant that Crane was very likely killed by one of his many former lovers or one of their furious male relationships. Such scandalous details ensured that the incident caught the public's attention and remained in the media.

But it was not one of these women that authorities began to focus on the investigation. Crane's longtime friend John Henry Carpenter became the main suspect after a trace of blood was found in his rental car. But the sample wasn't conclusive, so he wasn't charged with nothing to discriminate against Carpenter. In 1990, the incident was reopened after rediscovering evidence photographs potentially showing the human organization of the rental car, further supporting Carpenter's charges. Carpenter was charged with first-degree murder and was tried in 1994. However, with no real tissue sample, Carpenter was acquitted for lack of evidence.

On November 14, 2016, local reporters still interested in the case were allowed to submit blood samples for more advanced DNA analysis, and then neither of the two sequences identified in the sample Or it turned out to not match any of the carpenters. Thus, the police's most promising suspects have been further exonerated and the case remains unresolved, with no lead other than hundreds of named or unnamed crane sexual cases.

13 CHICAGO TYLENOL MURDERS

On September 29, 1982, 12-year-old from Chicago, Illinois, Mary Kellerman died suddenly after drinking a super-strong Tylenol capsule. Later that day, in the neighboring Chicago suburbs, a man named Adam Janus mysteriously died after taking the same medicine. Two members of his family also died shortly after taking Tylenol. It took less time for authorities to discover the relationship between death and Tylenol, with three more victims following the same fate in the surrounding area. This strange series of deaths revealed that the Tylenol capsule was wrapped in potassium cyanide.

The bottles, all tampered with, came from different factories, but the victims were all in the Chicago area. In other words, the tampering was done inside the store, not at the production level.

Johnson & Johnson, the manufacturer of Tylenol, immediately cuts all Tylenol production and advertising and advised the public not to take drugs containing acetaminophen. After it was discovered that only the capsules were tampered with, the company offered to replace all purchased capsules. The incident soon implemented stricter standards to prevent drug tampering. Another major change is the change from capsules to solid caplets in the shape of capsules, as the capsules show no visible signs of tampering and are easy to tamper with.

When the investigation began, Johnson & Johnson received several letters from James William Lewis that he had tampered with the capsule and demanded a $1 million suspension. Since he and his wife lived in New York at the time and had nothing to do with Chicago, police were unable to find credible evidence to suggest that Lewis was actually the culprit. However, he was arrested for extortion and sentenced to 13 years in prison (in addition to additional years of prison for unrelated crimes). Other suspects appeared, but police were unable to connect any of them to the Tylenol killing.

After the 25th anniversary of the crime renewed public interest in the case, police received some new tips and regained old evidence. In 2009, they conducted another study of Lewis's house and later received a sample of Lewis's DNA for analysis, but found nothing further acquitting him. The FBI even called for DNA samples from "Unabomber," Ted Kaczynski, who was plagued by couples in the same area only in the previous years, but denied any involvement with potassium cyanide. Unfortunately, none of the new leads have stopped completely and the investigation continues.

14 COLONIAL PARKWAY MURDERS

The Colonial Parkway is a beautiful highway that runs through the Colonial National Historical Park in Southeast Virginia. The parkway is surrounded by woods and has far fewer doorways than regular highways. It was typically a quiet area, and no one expected the Parkway to be the setting for a horrific murder.

Kathy Thomas and Rebecca Dawski
On October 12, 1986, pedestrians saw the car down the embankment of the Colonial Parkway and disappeared from the road. They called a highway guard who arrived at the scene to make a gruesome discovery of the bodies of two young women in a car. Two women in the car were identified as Kathleen "Cassie" Thomas, a 27-year-old graduate of the Naval Academy, and Rebecca Andowski, a 21-year-old student at the University of William and Mary. The couple had been missing since the evening of October 9 after being seen leaving the computer room. The two women were tied up with ropes and strangled, and the murderer slashed his throat deeply and cut off his neck. Rebecca's body was in the back seats of the car, and Cathy was in a hatchback. There was no evidence of sexual assault. Police believed the murder occurred elsewhere, and che body was dumped in the car because the car itself had little blood. They also ruled out robbery as a motivation, as both women's wallets were still there and no money or jewelry was taken. The killer tried to burn the car with gasoline, but he couldn't. The police thoroughly investigated it, but in the

end the incident calmed down.

David Knobling and Robin Edward

Things seemed to have returned to normal until September 22, 1987, when the body of another young couple was found along the James River, Virginia. The two remains, David Knobling (20) and Robin Edwards (14), have been missing since September 19. They met at the beginning of the day in the arcade and Robin was creeping up to meet David later that night. David's car was found in a parking lot by James River Bridge. The car had two pairs of underwear, shoes, and David's wallet, and ruled out robbery. The driver's side window was partially rolled down, and police made the perpetrators believe that they were, perhaps, in some uniformed officer. Both victims were shot, Robin was behind the executional style of the head, and David was shot twice, once on the head and once on the shoulder, as he had fled the murderer. Robin's pants were partially rounded, but police were not convinced that there was sexual assault because Robin and David were presumed to have had some sexual relationship. No murders had occurred on Colonial Parkway, but police said that both sets of victims were a couple who were murdered in or near the lover's lane area, with two locations approximately 30 minutes by car. I linked the incident because it was only a distance away. Once again, despite the police's best investigation efforts, the case has calmed down. No murders had occurred on the Colonial Parkway, but police said that both sets of victims were a couple who were murdered in or near the lover's lane area, with two locations approximately 30 minutes by car. I linked the incident because it was only a distance away. Once again, despite the police's best investigation efforts, the case has calmed down. No murders had occurred on the Colonial Parkway, but police said that both sets of victims were a couple who were murdered in or near the lover's lane area, with two locations approximately 30 minutes by car. I linked the incident because it was only a distance away. Once again, despite the police's best investigation efforts, the case has calmed down.

Cassandra Haley and Richard Cole

Within a year, another young couple was missing. On April 10, 1988, two students at Christopher Newport University, Cassandra Lee Haley (18 years old) and Richard Keith Cole (20 years old), went missing after joining a party together at Newport News. It was. It was the very first date of a young couple. The next day, Richard's car was found in the York River Outlook on the Colonial Parkway, about two miles from where Kathy and Rebecca were found. Almost all the clothes Cassandra and Richard were wearing were found in the car, along with Richard's and Cassandra's wallets, again motivated by robbery. Despite extensive research, their bodies were not found and the couple was presumed dead.

Daniel Lauer and Anna Maria Phelps

About a year and a half later, two more young people were missing near the Colonial Parkway. On the Memorial Day weekend of 1989, 21-year-old Daniel Lauer drove to his brother's house in Virginia Beach with his brother's girlfriend, Ana Maria Phelps (18). I-64. A car was found west of the highway, opposite the destination, confusing police. It is unknown if Anamari and David stopped and were killed at the rest of the stops, or if killed elsewhere and the murderer moved the car. Anna Maria's wallet was found in the car. Once again dominated by robbery. Their bodies were found by hunters on October 19th, a month later, on a logging road about a mile from the rest of the stop. The body was covered with a blanket of Daniel's car and was severely disassembled, making it impossible to determine the cause of death or the presence of sexual assault. Although the cause of death could not be determined, a stigma was found in Anamari's bone, suggesting that she had been stabbed to death. Like the other three cases, the case eventually cooled and the murderer was never tried.

Police attribute the killings of these eight people to the same murderer, as they are similar in each case. All victims were killed in or near the car. The first three were found in a place known for their lover's lane. No victim was robbed and sexual violence did not appear to be a motive in any case. The first and third murders were only a few miles away, and the second and fourth murders were committed about 30 minutes away from Parkway. However, some believe that these murders were not due to serial murderers' work, but to at least two or more murderers. Differences in killing methods are often pointed out. It seems that Kathy and Rebecca were strangled, their throats dissected, David and Robin were shot, and Anna Maria and Daniel were stabbed.

Detective Steve Spingora was asked to investigate the Colonial Parkway murder as a private detective. Sphingora believes that the murders of Kathy and Rebecca have nothing to do with other murders, and are in fact related to another double murder that occurred in Shenandoah National Park in 1996. A young couple, Julie Williams, 24, Lolly Winance, 26, was camping in the park on Memorial Day weekend. They were reported missing when they did not go home. Their bodies were discovered on June 1. They were tied up and nauseated, as were Kathy and Rebecca, and their throats were cut. Mr Spingola believes the two murders are hatred offenses committed by the same perpetrators.

Despite the theory that crime may not be connected, many believe that colonial Parkway killing is the job of serial murderers. Over the years, police have questioned 150 suspects in connection with these four cases, all of which have been arrested. In 2018, Cathy's brother Bill Thomas' Facebook page, Colonial Parkway Murders, found DNA in three of four crime scenes, potentially linking the case and leading to arrest. Revealed that there is. Hair found in Kathy's hand and biological samples found in Robin have not been tested yet, but advances in DNA technology and resources such as GEDmatch hope victim families will eventually be answered. doing.

15 D.B. COOPER HIJACKING

Dan "DB" Cooper became a legend on the eve of Thanksgiving in 1971. Since that night, police have failed to find out if he is dead or alive after jumping from plane to plane.

At around 4 pm on November 24th, a man named Duncooper entered Portland International Airport and bought a one-way ticket to Seattle Tacoma Airport for $20. He was assigned aisle seat, 18C, for the 4:35 pm flight. The plane does not include a pilot, Captain William Scott, co-pilot Bobra Tacuzak, flight engineer HE Anderson, and two flight attendants, Tina McCraw and Florence Schaffner.

A middle-aged, white man with no accent, in a dark suit and tie, Cooper drew little attention when boarding. After takeoff, Cooper gave Schaffner a note. At that time, men traveling alone were generally slipping phone numbers or hotel room numbers to flight attendants, so Schaffner put the note in his pocket and ignored it. The next time Cooper passed, it moved closer. He told her that he had read the note carefully and warned him that he was nodding into the suitcase and there was a bomb. Then Schaffner went to the galley and read the notes. She showed it to the other flight attendants and rushed into the cockpit to show the pilot with them. The pilot immediately contacted air traffic control after he read the note. They now contacted Seattle Police and notified the FBI. The FBI made an urgent call to airline president Donald Nyrop and said he should comply with Cooper's request. Without a doubt, Nyrop wanted to avoid the negative publicity caused by such a disaster.

Cooper instructed the flight attendants to return the memo and was wary of potentially guilty evidence. For this reason, the exact wording of his memo is unknown. Schaffner recalled that the handwritten ink notes required $200,000 in cash and two sets of parachutes. Cooper hopes to deliver these items when they arrive at Seattle Tacoma Airport and claims to blow up the plane if it fails to meet these demands. Everyone who read the notebook agreed that the phrase "Do not do any weird work" was included.

Cooper moved to the side of the window, so she was sitting in the aisle seat when Schaffner returned. He opened the suitcase wide enough so she could get a glimpse of the wire and the two cylinders, potentially the dynamite stick. He then instructed her to return to the cockpit and instruct the pilot to stay in the air until the money and parachute are ready. After receiving the message, the pilot announced, via an intercom, that the jet was turning before landing due to mechanical problems. Most of the passengers did not know hijacking.

Cooper was very accurate about his demand for money. He wanted $200,000 for a $20 bill. This weighs about 21 pounds. Using small banknotes adds weight and can be dangerous to his skydiving. The larger the bill, the lighter it will be, but the more difficult it will be to pass. He declared that he needed a random serial number invoice, not a serial. An FBI agent gave him a random serial number invoice, but confirmed that they all started with the code letter L.

Getting a parachute was much harder than raising $200,000. McCord Air Force Base in Tacoma offered to provide a parachute, but Cooper refused. He wanted a private parachute with a user-operated lip cord, not one issued by the military. The Seattle police finally contacted the owner of the skydiving school. His school was closed, but they persuaded him to sell four parachutes.

Cooper's takeover memo did not directly explain his plan to skydive from an airplane, but his request led the authorities to that assumption. He requested an additional parachute, so they assumed that he would take the passenger or crew with him as an aerial hostage. They considered using a dummy parachute in exchange for Cooper, but could not endanger the lives of civilians.

At 5:24 pm, the ground team had cash and a parachute, so we wirelessly contacted Captain Scott to let him know he was ready to arrive. After landing, Cooper ordered a taxi to a far bright place. He dimmed the cabin lights and ordered that no vehicles approach the plane. He also ordered those who bring cash and parachutes to be unaccompanied.

A Northwest Airlines employee drove a company vehicle near an airplane. Cooper ordered the flight attendant Tina McCraw to go down the stairs. The employee carried two parachutes to the stairs at one time and handed them over to McCraw. Next, the employee put the cash into a large bank bag. When the requirements were met, Cooper released 36 passengers and flight attendant Florence Schaffner. He did not release the other flight attendants Tina McCraw and the three men in the cockpit.

FAA staff contacted the captain and asked Cooper for permission to board the jet. Officials apparently wanted to warn him of the dangers and consequences of piracy. Cooper denied his request. Cooper asked McCraw to read an instruction card on how to operate the rear stairs. When he asked her about them, she didn't think she could lower them in flight. He said she was wrong.

Cooper chose this flight not only because of the location, but also because of the type of jet used. He was familiar with the Boeing 727-100. Cooper ordered the pilot to stay below 10,000 feet and maintain airspeed below 150 knots. Experienced skydivers can easily dive at 150 knots. The jets are lightweight and can fly at this low speed in 10,000 feet of dense air.

Cooper told the crew that he wanted to go to Mexico City. The pilot explained that at the altitude and airspeed he wanted to move, the jet couldn't move more than 1,000 miles using 52,000 gallons of fuel. With this in mind, they agreed to stop halfway to refuel in Reno, NV. Prior to leaving Seattle, Cooper ordered the jets to be refueled. He knew the Boeing 727-100 could capture 4,000 gallons of fuel per minute. After 15 minutes, when refueling was not done, Cooper asked for clarification. The fuel crew soon finished work. Captain Scott and Cooper have negotiated a low altitude route called Vector 23. This route allowed the jet to fly west of the mountain safely at the low altitudes required by Cooper.

Cooper instructed the cabin to depressurize the cabin. He knew that a person could breathe normally at 10,000 feet and that if the pressure inside and outside the cabin were equal, there would be no violent gusts when the rear stairs were lowered. After all the flight details were known, the plane took off at 7:46 pm.

After takeoff, Cooper ordered the flight attendants and the rest of the crew to stay in the cockpit. There was no peephole or remote camera installed at the time in the cockpit door, so the crew had no idea what Cooper was doing. At 8pm, a red light warned that the door was open. On the intercom, Scott asked Cooper if he could do anything. He was angry and answered "No!" This was the last word I heard from Duncooper.

At 8:24 pm, the jet loosened the nose after the nose first lowered, then the tail end descended. Scott paid attention to where the submergence occurred, near the Lewis River, 25 miles north of Portland. The crew assumed that the rear stairs were down and Cooper had jumped up. But they didn't confirm their assumptions because they didn't want to violate his command to stay in the cockpit.

At 10:15 pm, the jet plane landed in Reno, Nevada. Scott talked about the intercom, and because there was no reply, he opened the cockpit door. The cabin was empty. Cooper was gone, along with money and his belongings. The only item left was the second parachute.

No one ever heard from Cooper. All subsequent investigations have failed to prove if he survived his fateful jump. During the hijacking, police tracked the plane and attempted to wait for someone to jump. Originally they used F-106 fighters, but these planes were built to run at high speeds up to 1,500 MPH, and proved useless at low speeds. Police then chose the Air Force National Guard Lockheed T-33, but before Cooper could catch up with the hijacked plane, Cooper was already jumping.

Due to the bad weather that night, police were unable to search the property until the next day. During Thanksgiving, and for the next few weeks, police conducted an extensive investigation that failed to find evidence of hijackers or parachutes. Police began searching for a criminal record named Dan Cooper in case the hijacker used his real name but no luck. However, one of their early results proved to have a lasting impact on the incident. An Oregon police record named DB Cooper was discovered and was considered a suspect. He was immediately cleared by police, but a keen and careless member of the press mistakenly confused the man's name for the alias given by the hijacker. This simple mistake was repeated by another reporter citing the information, and so on, until the entire media used catchy Monica. Therefore, the original "Dun" Cooper became known as "DB" in the rest of the study.

The piracy charges were filed in 1976 and continue to exist. On February 10, 1980, an eight-year-old boy found a serial number in a bundle of $20 bills, a number that matched that of the Cooper Vault on the Columbia River. Some people believe that this evidence helps support the theory that Cooper did not survive. The discovery of these bundles has led to new searches around the area. But a mountain eruption. St. Helens, May 18, 1980, probably destroyed the remaining clues about the Cooper case.

Over the years, many have acknowledged that they are Dan Coopers. The FBI has quietly investigated some of these cases, but none are useful yet. They check the fingerprints of people who confess against unknown prints collected from hijacked planes. So far, none have matched.

In August 2011, Marco Cooper claimed that Dan Cooper was her uncle's LD Cooper. Mara claimed to have heard the conversation that the money problem was over, and had taken over the plane. But she also explained that money was never recovered because his uncle lost it while he was jumping. Many have identified Duncooper as one of their relatives for many years, but

Mara Cooper's claims seem to be closest to the truth. But this theory has not yet been considered by the authorities.

In July 2016, the FBI officially announced that it will not allocate active resources to continue its investigation of DB Cooper. This did not mean that they resolved the case of Cooper's identity. The main theory by investigators is that Cooper did not actually survive his jump. His extensive knowledge of the plane's system led police to believe that he was a professional skydiver, but he crossed the ruthless Washington wilderness in midwinter while wearing business casual attire. Thus, such a surge in weather conditions has been concluded since then, and there is no risk to the experts to be silly. The fact that the ransom matching bag turned out to remain on the stream further supports the theory that he did not survive.

16 WHO KILLED DIAN FOSSEY?

Dian Fossy, also known as the Gorilla Girl, is a well-known primatologist working in the state of Ruhengeri, Rwanda, and the author of the best-selling book "Gorilla in the Mist." She was found dead in her isolated hut in the mountains. Visoke's research site died on December 27, 1985, when he was hit by Machete on his face.

Fossey has established a reputation as a kind woman among followers, but to her enemies she can be ferocious. In his life in Rwanda, Fossi confirmed that poachers had devastating effects on the wildlife of the region. Rwanda officials, who were supposed to enforce the law, often participated in poaching. Her focus began to shift from research to protection, fighting poachers, and militarily protecting the gorillas she studied. According to ex-colleague Bill Webber, she tortured and kidnapped her enemy. Indeed, many of her own writings confirm this. She has also earned her reputation as a witch. She often used the locals' fear of magic to scare them away from hunting in their study zone.

Despite apparent hostility between Fossey and the locals, police first saw members of her research team as their main suspects. Shortly after her death, all her staff were arrested and slowly released due to lack of evidence. A few months later, after clearing him for the first time, Rwandan officials suddenly charged one of the researchers, Wayne McGuire, with the murder of Fossey.

However, he was conveniently informed of the charges and was able to leave the country and return to the United States where prosecution was not pursued. For this reason, many believe that this "resolution" is a plot by Rwandan investigators and use McGuire as a scapegoat to protect poachers and officials. In 2001, Mr. Protice Zigiranyirazo, the governor of the Ruhengeri region in 1985, was later accused of ordering the death of Rwanda. The case remains unresolved to this day. Fossy is in Rwanda. Gorilla is buried in the cemetery of her research site.

17 JACK THE RIPPER

Ripper Jack was a notorious serial killer in the East End of London in 1888. He killed a prostitute in the Whitechapel district of London. The Ripper case is famous. The criminal remains unidentified. Today it remains one of the largest unsolved cases in the world.

Mary Ann "Polly" Nichols was the first victim. On August 31, she was killed and amputated. Annie Chapman was killed just a week later. Elizabeth Stride and Catherine Ed Weson were killed at the end of September. Mary Jane Kelly was killed in November. These five murders are ripper murders, of which only five have been identified, but more are theorized.

Based on severe atrocities on the body of his victims, he was believed to be a man with some experience in butchery or medicine.
One of the things that has captivated the world today about the ripper murder is the mystery of classicity. It's an open and shut murder, but it lacks one element, the solution. He killed five women for no apparent reason, then disappeared, and never again.

Even today, London still benefits from the ripper phenomenon, with a wealth of guided walks and ripper memorabilia at the murder scene. Many books have been written on this topic, and there are several films based on the tradition of Jack the Ripper.

18 WHAT HAPPENED TO JIMMY HOFFA?

The leader of the notorious workers and chairman of the Team Stars International Brotherhood from 1958 to 1971 mysteriously disappeared on July 30, 1975.

Hoffa gained more power because the union was closely linked to organized crime, but was also associated with some dubious practices. Hoffa was sentenced to 13 years for jury tampering, postal fraud, and bribery, but was pardoned in 1971 by President Richard Nixon on condition that he was not involved in union activities. Still, by the time of his disappearance, Hoffa was already trying to rebuild the team star's support base in Detroit, pissing off those who took power during his absence.

Despite the hundreds of wild theories about what happened to Jimmy Hoffa, only a few details of his disappearance were actually confirmed. On July 30, 1975, Hoffa left his home in the green Pontiac Grandville to meet two mobs, Anthony Jacaron and Anthony Probenzano. , At 2:00 pm at Mathew Red Fox Restaurant, Hoffa called his wife and said she hadn't appeared yet. When Hoffa didn't go home, his wife reported that he was missing. His car was found in a restaurant with no sign of where Hoffa went. The last time he saw him alive was a trucker, who saw Hoffa riding Marquis Marquis alongside other unidentified men, who almost collided with the truck as he left Red Fox. I saw it. The description of the vehicle was exactly the same as that owned by

Hoffa's friend Chucky O'Brien and owned by Anthony Jacarone's son. At the time. Authorities struck the vehicle on 21 August, when he had already suspected O'Brien in a recent case with Hoffa. The trail has just cooled. By 1982, the FBI had declared Khofa's dead, but had no idea where his body was.

In 2001, the hair found in O'Brien's car was DNA tested, confirmed to be Hoffa's hair, and finally the original theory that he was at least in the car. Investigative gangsters seem to turn new pages in 2004 Frank Sheeran releases his biography and claims he was able to prove he was a murderer: O'Brien put them all in Detroit's house. Driven, Sheeran may still find evidence of blood inside Hoffa and Shot. Analysis revealed that the blood found in the house was not from Hofa, and police returned to its original condition.

Several other sites were searched for the next few years, such as horse farms and under the gang's garage, but nothing was found. The FBI said the most likely explanation was that the new team star's leadership ordered a hit on Hoffa, preventing his return to union politics. At this point his body is unlikely to be discovered.

The people continue to be fascinated by their disappearance. The mafia's underworld's wild charm and wild conspiracy theory fuels a reference to Jimmy Hoffa's disappearance in pop culture to date. In 2006, the FBI released an official comprehensive casebook (known as Hoffex Memo) from 1976, reiterating worldwide interest. Leads will continue to be presented and investigated by the FBI, but they are not yet close to finding out what actually happened to Hofa on July 30th.

In an interesting bookend, Hoffa's son James Hoffa became president of International Team Stars in 1998.

19 THE UNSOLVED DEATH OF AMERICAN BEAUTY PRINCESS JONBENÉT RAMSEY

Early in the morning of December 26, 1996, John and Passy Ramsey woke up and discovered that his six-year-old daughter, John Bennett Ramsey, was missing from his bed at home in Boulder, Colorado. Patsy and John were up early to prepare for the trip, and a ransom note was found on the stairs demanding $118,000 for the daughter's safe return home.

Despite the memo's warning that he should not involve the police, Patsy immediately called them, friends and family to assist John Beneramsey in his search. Police arrived at 5:55 am and found no signs of forced invasion, but ultimately did not search the cellar where her body was found.

There were many investigative mistakes before John Bene's body was found. Only John Bene's room was surrounded, which could allow friends and family to roam the rest of the house, pick things up, and destroy the evidence. Boulder police also shared the evidence they found with Ramsey, delaying the conduct of informal interviews with their parents. At 1 pm, the detective instructed Mr Ramsey and his family friends to walk around the house to see if there were any problems. The first thing they saw was in the basement, where they found John Bene's body. John Ramsey immediately picked up the daughter's body and took him upstairs, but unfortunately disturbed the crime scene and destroyed potential evidence.

At necropsy, John Bennett Ramsey was found to have died from strangulation due to strangulation in addition to skull fracture. Her mouth was covered with duct tape and her wrists and neck were wrapped with white cord. Her torso was covered with a white blanket. There was no definitive evidence of rape, as sexual assault occurred but no semen was found on the body and the vagina appeared to be wiped clean. The makeshift attic was made from a length of cord and a piece of paintbrush from the basement. The coroner also discovered what was thought to be a pineapple in John Bene's stomach. Her parents don't remember giving her the night before she died, but she had a bowl of pineapple in the kitchen and a fingerprint of her 9-year-old brother Burke. But it made little sense because time cannot be attributed to fingerprints. The Ramseys claimed that Burke had slept in his room overnight, with no other physical evidence to reflect anything else.

There are two popular theories in the Ramsey case. Family theory and intruder theory. The initial survey focused on the Ramsey family for a number of reasons. Police felt that the ransom note was so long that it was written from Ramsey's house using a pen and paper, so it demanded the nearly exact amount John received as a bonus earlier that year, so police felt it. It was In addition, the Ramseys were reluctant to cooperate with the police, later saying that they feared the police would conduct a thorough investigation and not target the simple suspects. However, all three close relatives were questioned by investigators and compared handwritten samples to the ransom letter they submitted. Both John and Burke have been removed from the suspicion of writing notes. Much has been done that Patsy can't definitively clear with hand-written samples, but this analysis was not further supported by other evidence.

Despite the growing number of suspects, the media quickly focused on John Bene's parents, who spent years in the harsh light of the public eye. In 1999, a Colorado grand jury voted to prosecute Ramsey for child risk and impediment to murder investigations, but the prosecutor refused to prosecute, feeling that the evidence did not exceed reasonable allegations. John Bennett's parents were not officially nominated as murder suspects.

Alternatively, the intruder theory had much physical evidence to support it. Next to John Bene's body was a print of boots that belonged to no one in the family. The windows in the basement, which were most likely to be intruders, were also broken. In addition, there was DNA from a drop of blood from an unknown man found in her underwear. It was plausible that the intruders carried John Bennett downstairs without waking up the family because the floors of Ramsey's house were carpeted.

One of the most famous suspects was John Kerr. He was arrested in 2006 after confessing that he had accidentally killed John Bennett after administering a drug to her and sexually assaulting him. Karl found that the drug was not found on John Bennett's system, and police were unable to confirm that he was in Boulder at that time, and the DNA did not match the profile generated from the sample found, so the final Was dismissed as a suspect.

Much of the recent investigation into the case revolves around DNA profiles developed from samples found in her underwear and touch DNA later developed from her long John. Her underwear profile was entered into CODIS (National DNA Database) in 2003, but no match was identified.

In 2006, Boulder Attorney Mary Lacy took over the case. She agreed with the federal prosecutor that the theory of intruders is more plausible than Ramsey, who kills their daughters. Under Lacy's direction, the investigators created a DNA profile from the long John tactile DNA, the DNA left behind by skin cells. In 2008, Lacy detailed the DNA evidence and issued a statement accusing the Ramsey family entirely.

"The Boulder Prosecutor's Office does not consider Ramsey families such as John, Passy, and Berk Ramsey to be suspects of the case, which significantly increases the exorbitant value of previous scientific evidence. This is because I recently obtained scientific evidence, and in this case I would like to thank you enough for the other evidence.

Local, national and even international publicity focus on the killing of John Bennett Ramsey. Many members of the public have come to believe that one or more Ramseys, including her mother, father, or her brother, are responsible for this brutal murder. These allegations were not based on court-tested evidence. Rather, they were based on the evidence reported by the media. "

In 2010, the case was officially reopened, refocusing the DNA sample. Further testing has been done on the sample and experts believe that the sample is actually from two people rather than one. In 2016, it was announced that DNA would be sent to the Colorado Bureau of Investigations to be tested in a more modern way, with authorities wanting to develop a stronger killer DNA profile.

In 2016, CBS aired the John Bennett Ramsey case, suggesting that his nine-year-old brother Burke was a murderer, despite being cleared by DNA evidence to prove the intruder's existence. Burke filed a $750 million lawsuit against CBS for defamation. The lawsuit was settled in 2019 and the terms of the settlement were not disclosed, but his lawyer said the lawsuit was "successfully resolved to the satisfaction of all parties."

The case of John Bene's murder remains open as it is still open.

20 WHO MURDERED THE MCSTAY FAMILY?

On February 4, 2010, Summer McStay, husband Joseph, and their little sons Gianni and Joseph Jr. disappeared from San Diego, California. The McStay family of four had a happy life, but recently moved to a new home. They were redecorating the house and turning it into a dream house. Joseph has a new design and installation of the fountain. This allowed me to spend more time with my family because of the flexible schedule and the ability to work from home.

On February 9th, family and business partners had never heard from Joseph on the 5th, they sent a colleague home to see if there was their family's beloved dog. When his partner arrived home, he found both dogs outside and had food in a bowl. So the family left the town and believed that someone was taking care of the dog.

On February 13, above, Joseph's brother went home when his family was not contacted within nine days. He found no signs of intrusion, except for windows that were partially open to enter the house. Inside, he found a relatively normal scene. The family moved into the house three months ago, unpacking and refurbishing. Joseph's brother couldn't find the signs of his family, so he was worried about his family, so he left a note for the person feeding the dog and asked him to call him. Later that night, he received a call from Animal Care, which was planning to take the dogs because they were left outside without food for over a week.

After all, summer and Joseph didn't arrange to feed anyone, because someone in animal care stopped by to feed the dog.

On February 15, 11 days after the family heard from the end, police searched McStay's family home. Although it looked normal to Joseph's brother, he was wary of the investigators. Due to lack of furniture and condition of the house during the renovation work, it was difficult to determine if there was any difficulty. However, the raw food left behind seemed to indicate that the family either hurried away or were going to return soon. There were no signs of unauthorized play or forced entry. There was no evidence to identify where the family went or why they left.

Earlier in the week before the family disappeared, Summer was planning to visit her sister, who recently had a baby. In addition, a family friend helped paint the house and went home on Saturday, February 6 to finish the job. The family didn't seem to have a plan to leave that day. On Thursday, February 4, the last day of contact with the Maxstays, Joseph attended regular work meetings. Mobile phone records show that he returned home after the meeting, and he kept calling until evening.

On the evening of February 4, investigators interrupted the investigation because a neighbor's security camera found McStays' car leaving home. The car never returned home. Investigators also discovered that the same car was towed on February 8 due to a parking violation near the Mexican border. The investigators immediately seized the car and searched for evidence. Inside, they found a relatively normal scene: there were some new toys, a child car seat was in that position, and the front seats were adjusted to the relative sizes of Summer and Joseph. There were no signs of cheating, but it was strange, very close to the Mexican border, as I was leaving my car and toys four days after leaving home. in addition,

Investigators discovered that neither of their family's cars had been traveling to Mexico for years, so they believed that the family did not drive to Mexico during the four-day bearer. Maxstays' family and friends did not expect to be on the Mexican border. In the summer, she said Mexico felt too dangerous and she would never be happy.

But new discoveries about border surveillance video have changed the direction of the investigation. Investigators discovered four people, similar to McStays, crossing the border around 7:00 pm on February 8th. Within 2 hours after parking the car in the nearby parking lot. The video shows a male adult and a child walking in front of a female adult with another child. The size of people seems to be similar to the Maxstay family. They had a mixed reaction when the family was called in to help identify people in the video. They realized that children and summer were people in the video, but Joseph's mother believed that if the guy in the video was Joseph, his hair would have been much bushier .. Otherwise, the family looked the same as Maxstays. They were dressed similar to McStays, and the kids wore hats similar to what they were pictured with. Investigators believed that the depicted family was probably Maxstays,

The investigators believed that it was not an indication that the family was walking past the border and suffering. Investigators searched the family's passport records and found that Joseph had a valid passport that had not been used before or after disappearance. The summer passport has expired and the detective was unable to find a record of her applying for a new one. In addition, neither child had a passport. The detective found one of the birth certificates left at home. It would have been impossible for McStays to travel to Mexico with insufficient paperwork. In addition, investigators have also discovered that summer has changed her name many times throughout her life. Renaming her alone is not ominous, but it has fueled many theories that summer was responsible for the disappearance. None of these theories have been confirmed. Summer may have used a different name, but there is no record of her other name's passport. The entire case completely confused the investigators and loved ones.

In April 2013, the San Diego Sheriff Office handed over the case to the FBI.

On November 11, 2013, the bodies of two adults and two children were recovered in the California desert. Two days later, the body was identified as the McStay family. The dead were murdered.

On November 5, 2014, ChSt Merritt, McStay's business associate, was arrested and charged with four murder charges after DNA was found inside McStay's car. The prosecution claims that Maxstay had gained merit and was killed by merit. The benefits are documented as the writing of checks for a total of $21,000 in McStay's business account after McStay has gone missing. Merit used that money to fuel gambling addiction at a nearby casino, losing thousands of dollars. The Merit trial has been postponed numerous times due to repeated firings of lawyers alleging the merit and has passed five times between November 2013 and February 2016. , Merit remained imprisoned without bail. The Merit trial finally began on January 7, 2019, and on June 10, 2019, a jury in San Bernardino County pleaded merit to the crime of murdering the McStay family. As a result, he may face the death penalty.

21 ARCHBISHOP ÓSCAR ROMERO BECOMES A SAINT, BUT HIS DEATH STILL HAUNTS EL SALVADOR

Oscar Arnull Forome Lau Gardames was a Roman Catholic priest in El Salvador who was assassinated on March 24, 1980.

The Oscar was ordained in 1942 and was promoted to Archbishop of San Salvador in 1977. He became a strong defender of the poor and called for the right thing to do. As Romero became more popular, people started listening to his sermons on the radio. He condemned the war between El Salvador and the leaders who created it. People called him a "voiceless voice" because he told what nothing else could do, and told the truth about injustice.

There was a coup in 1979. This means overthrowing the government. Unconstitutional seizure of power, usually by a dictator, army, or political faction. Initially Romero endorsed it, but persecuted the Catholic Church and asked the United States in 1980 to help with the famous open letter to Jimmy Carter.

Romero, who celebrated Mass on March 24, 1980, was shot dead in a chapel. No one was convicted of this vicious crime, but the United Nations Commission on Truth in El Salvador did its own investigation and concluded that it was given by Robert Dawson. D'Aubuisson was the leader of the Death Squad and a far-right politician. In 1997 Romero was given the title of servant of God by Pope John Paul II.

22 WHO KILLED TUPAC SHAKUR?

Tupac "2Pac" Shakur is one of the most popular rappers in the past and even now. Born in New York City in 1971, he moved to Maryland with his family at the age of fifteen. There he was able to develop his artistic talent by attending the Baltimore School of Arts, where he acted, wrote poetry, learned music, and often his class under the stage name MC New York. Wrapped for a mate Two years later, his family moved to California again. There he attended Leila Steinberg's poetry and performance class, and soon became his mentor and manager. Steinberg gave Tupac a big vacation in 1989. At that time, she introduced him to fellow manager Atron Gregory and the successful hip-hop group Digital Underground. Tupac has toured and recorded for several years before releasing his first solo album in 1991.

Shaqour initially signed with Intersope Records, but is increasingly involved with Death Row Records in Marion "Suge" Knight, known for his violent tactics and roles in the rapfade of "East Coast vs. West Coast". became. Deslow boasts California strong artists such as Tupac, Dr. Dre, and Snoop Dogg, and East Coast label Sean "Puff Daddy/P. Diddy Combs' Bad Boy Records is based on Christopher's "Notrias Big" Wallace. Was the home of such New York artists. Tupac was initially intimate with Wallace due to its New York roots, but the competition between the labels increased and soon the two reversed each other, with fatal consequences.

Shakur was on trial for sexual violence when he went to Quad Studios in New York on November 30, 1994 to record a song with Christopher Wallace and Sean Combs. While Wallace and Combs were upstairs, Tupac and his companions walked into the lobby of the recording studio where they were struck by a gun and robbed by three men. Shakur was shot five times to protect himself. He survived and arrived the court the next day, where he was sentenced to 1.5 to 4.5 years in prison.

While in prison, Shakur came to the conclusion that Wallace and Combs set up an attack and deliberately invited him into the studio as a setup. Wallace vehemently denied the claim, but the incident fueled rivalry and tensions steadily increased. Tupac was released from prison after nine months in prison, at which point he officially joined Sugenite and signed Deslaw Records. The shore-to-coast confrontation is even more hostile than it was before, as Tupac is again free to record.

On September 7, 1996, Shakur, Knight, and several bodyguards participated in Mike Tyson's battle at the MGM Grand in Las Vegas. A quarrel exploded when in the hotel lobby, a man named Orlando Anderson, a member of the Gang The Clips, California, recently robbed a fellow Deathlaw member (associated with a blood rival gang). .. In retaliation, Shackle led his group to attack Anderson, continuing until the fight was stopped by hotel security.

Later that night, the Death Row group headed to the club with Shakur in the passenger seat of a black BMW driving at night. A white Cadillac pulled up near them and fired several shots. Shakur was beaten four times in the chest, and one bullet scratched the knight's head. Shakur was taken to a hospital where he survived for 6 days and had several surgeries. Finally, on September 13, 1996, Shakur succumbed to his wounds.

Several theories have been published regarding the identity and motives of murderers. The most accepted by law enforcement is Anderson chasing Shakur after Wallace agreed to pay $1 million for the hit. Unfortunately, co-operation with police by both gang members was minimal, so police were unable to clearly identify

Anderson as an archer. Anderson was killed in an unrelated gang fire two years later, still innocent, and was not accused of Shakur's death.

Others believed that Squenite was behind the hit, as Shakur had accumulated litigation costs, and Knight believed that Shackle was more valuable in selling posthumous albums than Shackle was alive. maybe. In 2017, Knight himself added yet another theory and said in an interview that he believed that his shooting was actually intended to attack him as part of the Death Row coup planned by his ex-wife.

Sadly, without the help of a witness, and Anderson is no longer alive, Shakur's killing remains unsolved.

23 CHRISTOPHER "NOTORIOUS B.I.G." WALLACE

On March 9, 1997, famous rapper Christopher's "Notorious BIG" Wallace was shot dead in a drive-by shooting game. Despite problems with the law due to drug trafficking throughout his childhood in New York, Wallace became one of the world's most influential rap artists shortly after being discovered by Sean' Puff Daddy/P. He started recording with Diddy Combs, Combs label Bad Boy Records, and shortly after he was between Bad Boy Records and Marion "Suge" Knight's California-based Death Row Records label. It becomes the center of the rival of the famous "East Coast vs. West Coast" rap industry.

Wallace was inspired by the overnight rap sensation Tupac Shakur, whose solo album debuted just three years before Wallace, cementing him as one of the most influential rappers to date. .. Shakur was a West Coast artist, but he and Wallace have made a close friendship. It continued until Shackle was robbed and shot in the lobby of Bad Boy's Quad Recording Studio on November 30, 1994. Wallace and Combs invited Tupac to the studio. With them recording the song and being on the second floor at the time of the attack, I became convinced that Shakur organized the whole thing as part of the growing competition between labels. After this incident, feudalism became increasingly hostile, focusing on the round-trip jab between Knight and Comb, and Wallace and Shakur. The tension grew when September 7th, 1996, when Shakur was shot dead in Las Vegas. It was unclear whether the shooting was part of a coastal competition, or the result of the seemingly unrelated Shakur battle, but damage did. Death Row's affiliates were furious and thought that some of the Bad Boys were unquestionably responsible.

Just six months later, Wallace was in Los Angeles, touring at the 1997 Soul Train Music Awards, promoting the release of his new album, Life After Death. After attending the Vibe Magazine Party at the Petersen Automotive Museum in Los Angeles on the evening of March 8, 1997, Combs and Wallace's aides departed from three GMC suburbs and returned to the hotel. The Wallace car was parked at the crossroads, but was ambushed by two cars. Wallace pulled up the seated passenger, speeding up after four shots. He died shortly after midnight on the 9th.

The Wallace killing remains officially unresolved. Unlike the Tupac Shakur murder, which police could not track because of the lack of co-operation with the parties involved, many witnesses were willing to provide information about the attack on Wallace. The account agrees that the archer is a black man, driving a white Toyota Land Cruiser and wearing a blue suit and bow tie like members of Islamic countries would wear. For some reason, police were unable to proceed with the investigation, despite the overwhelming possibility that the firing was ordered by Suge Knight in retaliation for the deaths of these promising leads and Shackle. This is in line with existing rumors that LAPD members have been secretly repaid by Death Row Records, providing personal security during off hours. While one witness, Combs bodyguard and other guest alleged that the shooter was involved with a LAPD police officer there and was directly involved in the LAPD's involvement in the Wallace killing, Testified to have seen the stalks and wallace of the person at the VIBE party. However, the department concentrated the investigation on its relationship with the Crips street gang until the incident cooled.

Until 2005, when Wallace's family filed a lawsuit against LAPD for being involved in Wallace's firing, none of these police charges occurred. This was declared tort when the plaintiff's main witness fell, but the judge conspired with a prisoner official and conspired with several corrupt police officers who conceal the evidence of the case. Said there was sufficient evidence, including the identity of the suspect. The family filed a complaint again in 2007, but was rejected a second time because of procedural expertise.

In 2011, the FBI made the original case file publicly available. This included an autopsy report showing that only one of the bullets was deadly, even if Wallace was shot four times.

24 INSIDE THE MYSTERIOUS DISAPPEARANCE OF NATALEE HOLLOWAY

When Natalie Holloway (born October 21, 1986) was missing during a high school graduation trip to Aruba, hundreds of volunteers, Alba's investigators, FBIs, and Dutch soldiers to find the missing girl. United in their efforts to create an international enthusiasm. Despite witnessing some of her whereabouts the night before her disappearance, Natalie was not found and is now presumed dead. Ten different people were arrested during the investigation, all later released, and no one has been formally prosecuted.

disappearance

Natalie Holloway was reported missing on May 30, 2005 after failing to report to the airport to return from Aruba. Her luggage and passport were still in the hotel room. Her classmates and friends reported that she had seen her last leave Carlos Charlie's restaurant and nightclub in Oljanedstad. Three men were interrogated and said they had dropped Nathalie at the hotel and forced the police to finally release it without specific evidence of opposition. However, in their subsequent changing stories and additional witness testimony, the men were each further arrested several times during the investigation. The main suspect in the case remains Van der Slut.

The Natalie Holloway survey was extensive. During the first few days of the investigation, the Government of Alba gave the holidays thousands of Albanian civil servants on holidays to help the investigation. Fifty Dutch Marines were also deployed on the island to clear Natalie's coastline, and three Dutch F-16s were specially fitted with infrared imaging devices to scan the newly dug tomb land. Did. Despite the $3 million spent on their efforts and investigations (more than 40% of Alba's police operating budget), Nathalie's body was never recovered.

Beth denounces investigations charged with bribery, cover-ups, and corruption, and continues to want her daughter returned. He then helped establish the Natalie Holloway Resource Center, providing assistance and support to recently missing families and advising the public on safe travel.

development of
There are many theories about what actually happened to Holloway. Joran van der Slut changed the story of the event several times. It was recorded that he and Holloway spent some time at the beach, which left her alone at her will, after he and the Carpeaux said they had dropped Holloway to her hotel. In a later interview, Van der Sruth claimed that he had sold Holloway as a slave, and subsequently withdrew his testimony.

In March 2010, Van der Sruth forced $25,000 from Natalie's mother, Beth, demanding that money be remitted to his account in exchange for the site of Natalie's ruins. After receiving the money, he revealed the location, but the investigators found nothing there. Shortly thereafter, on May 30, 2010, he was arrested in Peru for the murder of a woman named Stephany Flores, who was found strangled in a hotel room. After confessing the crime, he was sentenced to 28 years in prison and may then face delivery to the United States for being charged with extortion.

In 2012, a petition declaring Natalie's father from her legal death was approved and signed by Judge King. Beth Twiti opposed the petition.

25 THE CRIMES OF BETTY LOU BEETS

Born in North Carolina, Betty Loubeatz claimed to have had hearing loss at age 3 due to measles and at the age of 5 had been sexually abused by his father and a few neighbors.

She was 12 years old and looked after her younger brother when she was admitted to the facility. At the age of 15, she married Robert Franklin Branson. After the first year of marriage, Betty claimed the relationship was abusive and the couple separated. However, after Betty's suicide attempt, the couple reunited. Robert left Betty and ended the relationship completely in 1969.

In 1970, Beats married Billy York Lane. Once again, Betty noticed a violent relationship and Billy broke Betty's nose during an argument. She shot him and retaliated. She was charged with attempted murder. But these charges were dropped when Billy first admitted that he had threatened her life. The couple divorced in 1972.

The following year, Betty dated Ronnie Surrell Cold, who married in 1978. The marriage ended a year after Betty tried to drive Ronnie.

It didn't take long for Betty to get married again. In 1979, she married her fourth husband, Doyle Wayne Baker. Her marriage to Baker was short-lived and in 1982 she moved to her fifth husband,

Jimmy Don Beats.

In August 1983, Betty told her former marriage son to leave home because he was going to kill Jimmy. When her son returned home, he discovered that Jimmy had been shot dead and helped his mother bury the body in the yard of his Texas home. Betty then reported that her husband was missing. It was until 1985 that evidence brought the police back to Betty. Police searched Jimmy Don Beats's body and the body of her fourth husband, Doyle Weinbaker, while searching for her property. Both men had their heads shot with the same .38 caliber pistol.

Two of Betty's children testified to their mothers, but also acknowledged their involvement in the cover-up of the murder. Betty pleaded acquitted and claimed that her children had been murdered. Despite her allegations, Betty was convicted of beating the beet and sentenced to death. She had already been sentenced to death, so she never tried to kill Baker.

In February 2000, at the age of 62, Betty Loubeats at the Huntsville unit in Texas died of a fatal injection.

26 THE BLACK WIDOWS OF LIVERPOOL

Catherine and Margaret Flanagan came to Liverpool from Ireland in the late 1800s. They began the residence of Catherine's son, John Flanagan, guest Thomas Higgins and his then six-year-old daughter Mary, and his 14-year-old daughter Margaret and Patrick Jennings. They had enough boarders, but the sisters were still very poor. As they became more and more concerned about their financial situation, they became aware of the burial community in the Liverpool area. The Burial Society was not essentially a for-profit life insurance group. All members paid dues, and then money was given to those who lost their relatives to pay for the funeral. The sisters have found that cheap and minimal funeral services can make money from the life insurance offered by these societies.

The first victim was John, Catherine's son. To the outside world, a once healthy 22-year-old boy soon seemed to be ill, and it was that illness that killed him. Behind the closed room, Catherine was poisoning his son with arsenic. Catherine almost immediately collected money from the burial community.

This Margaret Flanagan became Margaret Higgins and married the guest, Thomas Higgins. One year after the couple married, eight-year-old Mary Higgins fell ill and her cohabitant died as early as two years ago. Once again, money was raised in what was partly considered a rude haste. Just a few months later, another guest, 16-

year-old Margaret Jennings, died. This is when suspicion has grown in the Liverpool area.

The last thing the sisters did was the murder of Margaret's husband, Thomas Higgins. Higgins died after two days of sudden illness, but sisters and doctors blamed him for drinking and attributed his death to dysentery. Thomas' younger brother Patrick was shocked and shocked to hear his death. When he heard of numerous deaths at home, he took it to himself to investigate it. He asked the coroner's office to do a complete autopsy. Then he contacted the police. Police countered the sisters in a pub in Liverpool, when Katherine slammed through the door in her funeral outfit. Margaret was arrested for killing her husband. Inspections by Thomas Higgins revealed traces of arsenic everywhere. This prompted the examination of another guest who met her sister's premature fate. All three had traces of arsenic in their bodies. A woman who admitted Katherine while the guest was staying at her house submitted her. On October 16, 1883, the sisters were charged with the murder of Thomas Higgins. Death sentence. On March 3, 1884, the sisters were hanged together. They are known as the Black Widow of Liverpool.

27 NOTORIOUS CONVICTED KILLER DIANE DOWNS

On the evening of May 19, 1983, Diane Downs entered the Emergency Room Bay in Springfield, Oregon. Her three children, Christie (8), Cheryl (7), and Danny (3), were in a bloody backseat. Emergency room staff declared Sheryl dead in the field and sent the other two to the hospital with life-threatening injuries. When asked about what happened, Downs explained the story of a man who flagged her from the side of a dirt road while her three children were sleeping in the backseats. He demanded her car, she refused, and he shot her children. After fleeing, she fled to the emergency room. During a struggle with a "hairy" man, she also took a shot on her left arm, which was not life-threatening.

While her children were still in the hospital, Downs conducted media interviews, telling strange stories and beginning to explain her innocence. Her story didn't fit. It was full of irrelevant details that undermine the legitimacy of the story. It didn't make much sense for her to take her children into the field of sight in the dark and to say they were sleeping. Police have begun investigating the Downs. They were able to find her secret journal describing the affair she had with the married man. The man she was involved in did not want children, so she looked at them as a burden.

The stroke impaired Christie's ability to speak, but she was able to begin telling police what she remembered about the night. Her story did not include seeing a "hairy" man. As a result, police arrested Downs in February 1984 and the trial begins in May of the same year. However, Downs was planning to get sympathy from the jury. She seduced the man along the mail route and was pregnant during the trial. Star witnesses were placed on a stand after all evidence was introduced to Downs. After months of physical and psychotherapy, Christie Downs was able to take the position and tell the jury who shot her. Downs was convicted and sentenced to 50 years in prison. She was able to give birth between the verdict and the verdict. A baby named Amy Elizabeth was adopted by another family and renamed Becky Babcock.

Just three years after her sentence, Downs managed to escape from the prison in Oregon where she was detained. Two weeks later, she was found in another prisoner's husband's house, a few blocks from the prison. She remains in prison today in a higher security facility in California. In 2008 and 2010 she was denied parole and had to wait 10 years before applying again.

28 BLACK WIDOW KILLER JILL COIT

Born and raised in Louisiana, Zircoite spent his "normal" American childhood. But at age 15, she decided to live with her grandparents in Indiana. Jill was said to be beautiful and smart and attracted many of the new high school boys, including Larry Eugene Inen. Jill soon fell in love with Larry, dropped out of school at the age of 17, and married Larry at the age of 18.

Almost a year after they got married, the couple divorced and Jill returned to Louisiana to get a high school degree. After graduating, she enrolled at Northwestern State University in Louisiana, where she met college student Stephen Moore. The couple married in 1964, and a year later Jill gave birth to a boy. Shortly after his birth, the couple separated.

One night while in the French Quarter, Jill fell into a wealthy man named William Clark Coit Jr. However, she and Koito were married before the divorce with Moore was confirmed. William adopted Jill's son and she gave birth to another son nine months after marriage. The Coit family moved to Texas for William's work. William traveled frequently and Jill was able to connect with many men. He knew of her escape and accused her of only marrying him for his money. On March 8, 1972, she filed for divorce, and on March 29, 1972, Jill reported that William had been killed. The detective believed that Jill was responsible for his killing,

After William's death, Jill moved to California. While in California, she persuaded his wealthy 90's man to "recruit" her. He died a year later and she received most of his property. After that, he moved to Donald Charles Brodie, the US Marine Corps Major who became his fourth husband. The couple divorced in 1975, two years after their marriage.

The fifth husband was Jill's lawyer, Lewis D. Dirosa, following the killing of his third husband, William Clark Coit. The couple married in 1976 in Mississippi. Separated several times during his marriage, Jill married Eldon Duan Metzger, Ohio during his separate separation in 1978. Jill traveled to Haiti and divorced Dilosa. However, this divorce was not legally recognized in the United States.

Jill divorced Metzger, but was still legally married to Dilosa when he married his seventh husband, Carl V. Steeley, in 1983. This divorce was not legal. But in 1985, Jill finally divorced legally.

By 1991, he moved to his eighth husband, Jerry Boggs, one of the richest men in Colorado. After eight months of marriage, he found out that she was still legally married to Carl Steeley and abandoned their marriage. Jill then divorced Steely legally and dated Michael Bacchus. During this time, she was also in a civil suit seeking $100,000 against Boggs.

In 1992 she moved to Las Vegas Nevada where she married Roy Carroll, her ninth husband. The couple moved to their hometown of Carroll, Texas. But by the end of the year they were divorced and Jill married Michael Bacchus.

One week after hearing Jill and Jerry in a civil suit on October 22, 1993, Jerry Boggs was shot dead and beaten to death in his Colorado home. A son from Jill and her marriage to Moore told police that he suspected that his mother had killed William Clark Coit and Gerry Boggs. He told police that he said he was going to kill Boggs, and that night he was killed, so she called him up and said, "Hey baby. ."

Jill Coit and Michael Bucks were arrested on December 23,

1993 and in 1995 they were sentenced to first-class murder and conspiracy to attempt murder.

29 THE STORY OF JUDY BUENOANO

Born in Judia Swelty, Judi Buenoano spent his early life in Texas where he was raised by his father and mother together with his two brothers and brother Robert. Her mother died when she was four. Judy and Robert were sent to live with their grandparents. After his father remarried, Judy and Robert moved to New Mexico to live with him and his new wife. She claimed her father and stepmother abused and starved her, forcing her to work as their slave. At age 14, he was sent to prison for two months after attacking his father, stepmother, and two stepbrothers. After her release, she chose to attend a reform school, and after graduating in 1960 she became a nursing assistant. A year later, she gave birth to her illegal son, Michael.

In 1962 she married Air Force officer James Goodyear. The couple lived in Orlando, where they raised their son and daughter, and Michael, who was adopted by James. A few months after James returned home from work in Vietnam, he was hospitalized in 1971 after suffering from mysterious symptoms. James died and Judy collected money from insurance. Later that same year, Judy's house fell into a fire and she collected additional insurance.

The following year she began dating Bobby Joe Morris and moved to Colorado in 1977. Judy and her children moved with him. Only a few months later, Bobby Joe was hospitalized after suffering from mysterious symptoms. The doctor released him.

However, he fell at home, was hospitalized, and died two days later. Judy was then able to raise money from the insurance policy she gave to her.

A few years later, Judy's son, Michael, was to join the US military and be stationed in Fort. Benning, Georgia. On his way to Georgia, he stopped to visit Judy at her home in Florida. Immediately after arriving in Fort. Benning, he began to show symptoms of poisoning, and doctors found high levels of arsenic in his blood. A few weeks later, Michael's arm and leg muscles were so atrophied that his hands were useless and he needed metal braces on his legs to walk. He was removed from the army and returned to his mother's home in Florida.

In May 1980, Judy took his sons Michael and James to a canoe on the East River in Florida. The canoe turned over. James and Judy were able to swim to the shore. But Michael, who wore heavy metal leg braces, drowned. After the accident, Judy raised $20,000 from Michael's military life insurance.

After Michael's death, Judy opened his hair salon and started dating Florida businessman John Gentry. The couple got engaged and in October 1982 Judy forced him to agree on a life insurance contract with each other. Judy also persuaded John to take a special vitamin. John didn't feel well from the vitamins. Instead, in December 1982 he became ill and was hospitalized. During his stay in the hospital, he did not take vitamins and felt better. However, he never doubted that Judy was addicting him.

In 1983, John was on his way to a liquor store when his car curiously exploded. During his recovery, police began to find some contradictions in Buenoano's background. Further investigation revealed that Buenoano was taking a gentle tablet containing arsenic. This caused suspicion and led to the discovery of her son, Michael, her first husband, James Goodyear, and her ex-boyfriend, Bobby Joe Morris. It was decided that each one was a victim of arsenic poisoning. Buenoano had not been investigated or suspected of their death until the car was bombed.

In 1984 Buenoano was convicted of Michael's killing and

Gentry's attempted murder. In 1985, she was convicted of the killing of James Goodyear. She was sentenced to 12 years in Gentry, life in Michael Goodyear, and death in James Goodyear. She was also convicted of numerous acts of grand theft and arson as a means of earning insurance money. She was suspected of several other deaths, including the 1974 murder in Alabama and her boyfriend Gerald Dosset's 1980 death. Her involvement in these deaths has not been proved, and by the time she was suspected, she was already on the death row in Florida.

Her motive, known as the "Black Widow," was considered greedy-she raised $240,000 reported on insurance. Buenoano has never admitted to killing. At the age of 54 in 1998, she became the first woman to be executed in Florida since 1848 and the third to be executed in the United States since the resurgence of the death penalty in 1976.

30 SUSAN SMITH: LEGACY OF A FILICIDAL MURDER

When Susan Smith's story was first broadcast to the public, she seemed to be a desperate distraught mother for the return of her two children. But the sympathy she gained quickly diminished as evidence began to emerge that she was responsible for the death of her son.

Susan Lee Vaughan was born on September 26, 1971 in Union, South Carolina. She had an insecure childhood. Her father committed suicide and she was abused by her stepfather for years. As a result, she began to suffer from depression and repeatedly tried to take her life. Following this, she went on to several hierarchies, including one that started with David Smith. When Susan became pregnant, the two eventually married, but even after the birth of the two boys, the relationship remained unabated, with negligence on both sides.

During their separation, Susan began to have a relationship with Tom Findlay, known as one of Union's most qualified bachelors. Together with Findlay, Susan finally believed that her life could have some stability, but she was wrong. Findlay did not want the responsibility of an established family. He was also not convinced that Susan's actions against their different backgrounds and other men fit into the committed relationship. He sent her a dear John's letter in October 1994 in a letter of the kind explaining all this, and Susan later found that she had never felt so alone in her life. Would say

On October 25, 1994, a crying Susan was found at the entrance to a residence near John D. Lake. She was carjacked and claimed that her son, 3 years old Michael and 14 months old Alex, were kidnapped during the crime. For nine days, she and David appealed to the press for a safe return of their sons, but to many acquaintances and authorities, something seemed unsuccessful.

Smith's story was full of holes, and she was different each time she was asked about the incident. She did some polygraph tests, but all were inconclusive. Many of her friends talked about how Susan kept asking if Finlay would come to see her, which is strange for a woman they should be upset by her missing children. I knew it was.

Close monitoring and nine days of media attention prompted Susan to confess. On the night of October 25, she took her two sons to the backseat, lonely and suicidal, running through the road. She drove to John D. Lake, initially planning to roll into the lake, but abandoned the plan and watched the car roll underwater at neutral. She was able to give the authorities a car location, and the scuba diver found it and the bodies of her two young sons. In her trial her defense team alleged that Susan had addictive personality disorder and severe depression, and she needed moral judgment in committing this crime due to the need for a stable relationship with Findlay. Claimed to have overcome. However, she was convicted in July 1995 for the murder case. The death penalty not given. Two prison guards have been fired after allowing sleep with Susan since her imprisonment, resulting in her being repeatedly relocated through the prison system. She is currently serving a prison at the Lease Correctional Facility in Greenwood, South Carolina, and is eligible for parole in 2024.

31 CASEY ANTHONY TRIAL

The jury selection began with the Anthony trial, 2011

On May 10, 2014, evidence of "decompression" was found. After a few months of research focused on Kaley's mother, Casey Anthony, the body of Kaley's skeleton was found near her home. All the while, Anthony repeatedly lied about his daughter's whereabouts.

The case for murder and misleading law enforcement against Casey Anthony began with the selection of a jury. Due to the large-scale publicity associated with the incident, this process took place in Clearwater, Florida, rather than in Orlando, where the crime took place, in hopes of finding an unscrutiny jury pool in the media. .. The jury pool began to shrink as the jury allowed many to go home for financial and family reasons. The jury has been quarantined for several months and may have been unable to do the family work or care for the jury.

Potential jury answers to some of the questions further narrows the pool. For example, preconceptions about cases based on media attention can influence decisions, as was strongly thought about the death penalty.

At this stage in a long-term controversial case, jury selection is a historic moment, but not the only aspect of the court that made history in the field of criminal investigation. The judge ruled that evidence of disassembly should be accepted. Evidence of this nature will first appear in a Florida court.

During the investigation, several witnesses, including police officers with experience of disassembled bodies, noticed the "disassembled" odor of Casey Anthony's car through the murder department. Air tests in the trunk were conducted by experts at the University of Tennessee, who hosted the body farm, and showed that there was a disassembled body in the car. The judge's ruling allowed these witnesses to testify this information before the jury.

See the full case timeline here. Learn more about the selection process for judges.

9-1-1 Call-May 16, 2011
If you're interested in a 9-1-1 call from Cayley's grandmother, Cyndian Sony, you can find those transcripts here.

Body disassembly-May 16, 2011
Click here for more information on body disassembly found in Casey Anthony vehicles.

Trial expected to start Monday, May 23, 2011
.. The trial requires 12 and a few alternates, and after a large number of juries were dismissed on the grounds that lawyers could bias the decision, including financial difficulties and personal reasons, the alternate Were less than originally planned. Nevertheless, Judge Perry planned to start discussions in the week of May 23 in Orlando. The trial lasted up to eight weeks, with the jury being in quarantine all the time.

Trial Now-May 25, 2011
Casey Anthony's trial began in the week of May 23, beginning with an opening statement from both the prosecution and defense attorneys. The prosecution said, as expected, only Casey Anthony was able to kill his daughter, Cary, but there was another theory on the part of the defense. Anthony's lawyer told the jury that Kaley's death was an accidental drowning and the one-month delay before her disappearance was reported when Casey and her father George

Anthony found the body. He said it was due to a panic. According to the lawyer, Casey's subsequent actions – lying to friends and family about her daughter's whereabouts and having parties at a local club – were the result of her lifelong practice of hiding her pain. They claimed that this practice was formed in her childhood because her father was sexually abused. George Anthony testified as the first witness of the trial,

Continuing the trial-May 27, 2011
On the fourth day of the long-awaited Casey Anthony trial, the prosecution continued to present a lawsuit against Anthony, along with a few more witnesses. In addition to continuing to emphasize that her daughter did not mention her disappearance after her disappearance, testimony began to outline the story given by the prosecution.

Witnesses claimed that after Kaley's disappearance, Anthony did nothing else and worked at the club, and Kaley was with his nanny. However, these witnesses also admitted under cross-examination that she did not seem to be a bad mother or to have abused Cary when she was seen with her daughter. It was

The main witness who witnessed on this day was Anthony's father, George. He explained that his hut was missing some gas cans, which he later confronted with his daughter. She took them out of the trunk of her car and returned them. This happened about a week after Cayley was last seen, but was told before anyone in the family knew she was missing. Anthony's former boyfriend Lazarus also testified about the gas can and said she helped her break into the hut and get it.

George Anthony had left duct tape on one of them before the gas cans were taken out, he said, the returned cans had no duct tape. According to the prosecution, this is a relatively unusual type of tape found on Kaley's body six months later.

Fragrance of Decomposition and Motivation for Murder-May 28, 2011
The prosecution continued testifying to Casey Anthony. They focused on Anthony's car because we heard the jury described

George Anthony about the smell of disassembly in the car as he drove the car from camp to home. It was left in the parking lot and towed two weeks ago. The towing company's manager also testified of the odor and said it was detected whether the door was closed or the car was closed, but much stronger. The decomposition of the human body was a very unique and recognizable odor to anyone who had experienced it, and the manager testified that he had that experience. George Anthony also claims to be familiar with stench throughout his time as a detective.

The prosecution has begun to address Antony's motives by trying to present text messages that show his true feelings about Antony's daughter. Cayley was confronted with his desire for a party-filled lifestyle and his relationship with his boyfriend Lazarus. Judge Belvin Perry questioned the evidence nature of these messages, suggesting that they would be unduly disadvantaged, so the prosecution withdrew attempts to introduce those messages.

Cary's Grandmother Testifies-May 30, 2011
Saturday May 28th The Casey Anthony trial session was short, focusing on Cindian Sony's testimony, Casey's mother. It was Cindy who finally reported that Kaley was missing a month after her last meeting, and her testimony focused on that month. Cindy described her repeated attempts to meet her granddaughter and various explanations for her daughter's absence of children. The description included a nanny named Zany who was taking care of Cayley while Anthony was attending a work session and a car crash while out in Tampa. Another explanation was that they were staying in a hotel with a wealthy suitor. These stories are inconsistent with previous testimony, and Anthony's lawyers suggested that Anthony's lies during this period were due to a habit of hiding her pain based on the history of abuse.

Casey's claim is disputed-June 2, 2011
Casey Anthony's testimony about her work and her boyfriend brought evidence of Anthony's deception. Anthony told his friends and family that he had a wealthy suitor, Jeffrey Michael Hopkins, who worked at Universal Studios. On that day, the jury heard from Anthony's acquaintance Jeff Hopkins and an employee of Universal. Hopkins said he knew Anthony at school, but had no

children and did not introduce Anthony to Kaley's nanny. The details of some other aspects and her story about him were not true, including their relationship, his work, and the place where he lived. Leonard Totra, an employee of Universal Studios, explained that he wasn't working at Universal while he was being questioned, witnessed, and argued by police about Anthony's work.

The testimony included a statement and an interview with Anthony after Cayley was reported missing, claiming that Cary was kidnapped by a nanny introduced by Hopkins. Investigators could not find the nanny described by Anthony. Anthony claimed that she did not come to the police after being abducted from fear. The defense's allegations that Cayley died of accidental drowning are clearly inconsistent with this original statement.

Hairy Kaley is found in a car-June 4, 2011
After witnesses testified that they smelled the decomposition odors from Casey Anthony's car, it was suggested that it was Cary's body that produced the odor of evidence. According to FBI's trace analysts, car hair is similar to that taken from Kaley's brushes. It also states that car trunk hair contains hair that remains on the scalp when the body begins to break down, a mark that was only found on the hair when the body started to break down. I will. Cary's similarity to hair was not an absolute distinction, as hair comparisons were not absolute to the individual and consisted primarily of color similarities. DNA present in the hair shaft was also tested, but this was not DNA that could be linked to a single individual.

Hair torn by roots can still contain nuclear DNA, whereas hair as seen in cars contains only mitochondrial DNA. Unlike nuclear DNA, mitochondrial DNA does not change between generations, but is passed directly from mother to child. This means that the DNA analysis of the hair only shows that it belonged to someone of Cary's maternal lineage, such as Cary, Cayce, or Cindian Sony.

Analysts explained that particular bands of hair were consistent with disassembly, but this observation is based solely on her experience, not a proven correlation.

Other interesting forensic evidence included an air sample taken from a car, showing signs of gas consistent with decomposition, and prosecution said Anthony killed his daughter with chloroform.

Evidence of disassembly ~ June 7, 2011
Testimony has so far focused on forensic evidence of the disassembly of Casey Anthony's car. After hearing from several eyewitnesses explaining the car's decomposed odor, the jury heard from experts that there was evidence of the same odor.

Some aspects of the odor of the trunk were presented. A trash bag was found in the trunk and was ruled out by a technician as the source of the stench seen by the witnesses. A highly trained corpse dog warned the torso, indicating that the body was stored internally. The jury heard from Arpad Vass, a forensic anthropologist who is doing research at a body farm on decomposition.

Vass conducted chemical tests on trunk air samples, carpet samples, spare tire covers, and car wheel well shavings. Of the 30 or so chemicals that his study found to be important for human degradation, samples from Anthony's torso contained seven, two of which were counted as traces. There were only 5 types. He testified that these results show that only the decomposed relics can explain the core odor. We also testified that the sample contained high levels of chloroform. An important fact for the prosecution, Anthony claims to have used chloroform before choking her daughter.

Cary's Skeleton and Duct Tape Length Discussed-June 10, 2011
Earlier testimony focused on signs of disassembly from Casey Anthony's car body, while subsequent testimony focused on the body itself. Kaley Anthony's skeleton was discovered on December 11, 2008, and had been disassembled in the field in a garbage bag for up to 6 months. Duct tape was found in the mouth, which fastens the jawbone to the rest of the skull. The placement of duct tape was important in the prosecution's trial of misconduct.

Chief medical examiner Dr. Jan Garvaglia testified today that duct tape and Anthony did not report the disappearance of their daughter, in addition to cheating on how the body was placed in a "corrupted" state.

Further evidence includes overlaying Kaley's skull on her face to show the placement of duct tape prior to disassembly. Although potentially disturbing and thus unfavorable to the jury, Judge Perry granted this evidence because of its importance in the case.

Day 16 Bug occurrence-June 12, 2011
Jury members at Casey Anthony saw testimony from forensic entomologist Neal Haskell regarding evidence of insects. He explained that the insect species present in the body parts showed a long-term presence in the body and had been present since June or July before it was discovered in December 2008. It also explained that insects collected from the trunks of Anthony's cars demonstrated the existence of a short-term body before it was removed – meaning what earlier witnesses suggested throughout the week. Entomological evidence is the most accurate indicator of the time of death after the body has broken down.

A video showing Cayley's skull overlay with duct tape over his mouth was shown on the photo of her alive and laughing the day before, with a breakdown of what made the third week of the test so tragic. Added to the testimony.

Prosecutors Planning Rest-June 15, 2011
The Casey Anthony trial prosecutor has announced that it will complete the presentation of the case. The day before this announcement, Cayley's grandmother, Cyndian Sony, testified and talked about the Winnie the Pooh blanket and the canvas laundry bag found at the site where Cayley's ruins were discovered. On the day Anthony said, "I have said a tattoo. Casey Anthony finished a testimony from a tattoo artist-for Bellavita-Italian"

Petition to refuse prosecution ~ June 16, 2011
After the prosecution finished submitting the case, the defense counsel accused Casey Anthony of acquittal because the prosecution failed to fulfill the burden of proof. They said that Caylee Anthony was killed or had meditation. Judge Perry denied the allegations and defenses began to present their claims today.

Defense begins with DNA evidence-in charge of the Cary Anthony case on June 16, 2011

Forensics were interrogated by the defense before the jury. Crime scene investigators explained that no dirt was found on Casey Anthony's clothes when using another light source to check for bodily fluids. Later, a forensic DNA examiner testified that no blood was found in Anthony's torso. This is expected in situations where blood was not shed, such as suffocation, the prosecution's suggested cause of death. If the bag had a hole, the prosecutor claimed that the body was wrapped, and blood may have been found from the breakdown of the trunk's body in body fluids. Inspectors also explained that duct tape lacked definitive DNA evidence found in the ruins.

The defense has a well-known expert

Inviting and attacking forensics-June 20, 2011 Casey Anthony's lawyer hires two prominent forensics specialists after challenging the lawyer's entomologist's previous claims by the prosecution's entomologist. I invited you. First, forensic anthropologist William Rodriguez came out positively to testify about duct tape found near the ruins of Kaley Anthony, but this opinion was not pre-shared by the courts. .. The defense's dropout violated a court order, and Judge Perry threatened to defend the defense's lawyer, Baez, by disdaining "gameplay." Rodriguez is a co-founder of Body Farm, so his testimony places a great deal of weight on court proceedings.

The trial continued with testimony from Werner Spitz, a forensic pathologist. He criticized Kaley Anthony's death investigation, especially the performance of the medical examiner who said she should have opened her skull at the autopsy. He also said that duct tape was used to kill Cary, saying it was likely added to it after disassembly, rather than being placed on her nose and mouth at the time of her death. The prosecution's claim was denied. One reason for placing duct tape on the skull at that time may be to hold the jawbone while moving.

Forensic Botanist Testimony ~ June 21, 2011 The Casey Anthony trial continued its pattern by presenting evidence from a rather vague field within the forensic science when the forensic botanist testified. She talked about evidence of plants that existed where Cayley's ruins were found, and said the roots growing in the lump of hair could be weeks old. Therefore, the evidence of the plant, as the prosecution claims, does not suggest that the body had existed for six months, but it did not rule out the possibility. She also explained that the plant evidence found in Anthony's car did not appear to come from the site where the body was found.

After this, the session was canceled by Judge Perry, after discussions between the lawyer and the defense side to create a witness, after the first two were rejected. The next session was expected to be short.

Anthony Car Chloroform; Cindy Made Online Chloroform Searches ~ June 24, 2011
New prospects for prosecution are found in the form of a woman who shared prison time with Casey Anthony. April Whalen had an infant near Kaley in age. He died in a drowning accident in which Antley's defenses were very similar to what he proposed as the cause of Cary's death, including a child found by his grandfather. The prosecution investigated whether Whalen could be the inspiration for Anthony's story.

In addition to this possible blow to the defense case, one of the defense witnesses appeared to backfire. The defense counsel called on researchers to work with Vas, a forensic anthropologist who witnessed the state about the decomposition chemicals he found in Anthony's car. This witness explained that the chloroform they found in the trunk was surprising in such places, and that he and Bass could not find an explanation for its existence in the test. The testimony hit the defense, as the presence of chloroform could only support the prosecution case.

It was introduced because the trials were fairly forensic. Chemists testified that other chemicals were not clearly associated with decomposition, as the majority of air samples from cars contained gasoline and the presence of other natural sources. Forensic geologists talked about a soil sample of shoes brought back from Anthony's home, saying there is no evidence to associate shoes with the site where the ruins were found. The toxicologist explained that the hair mass found in the body showed no evidence of the drug, but was not tested for chloroform. Even more witnesses testified to chloroform and hair samples. Learn more about trial forensics here.

But it was the most testimony to the defense. Cyndian Sony was positive about saying he would search his computer for "chloroform," which was previously attributed to his daughter. She claimed she was looking for "chlorophyll" because of the health concerns of pets eating plants in the backyard, and she said she was looking for information about chloroform in relation to chlorophyll. However, there was some debate about her work record, which indicated that she was working when the search was done, so it was up to the jury to find her testimony convincing.

Sudden ability questions ~ 2011
On June 27, June 27, Judge Perry called a sudden break in the Casey Anthony trial before the jury entered the court and canceled all testimony that would otherwise have been presented. .. At that time, he had no explanation other than the occurrence of "legal problems." Possible reasons for the recession have been revealed: Anthony's defense argued that Anthony was not capable of trial. The allegation was filed and Perry was immediately examined by Anthony by three psychologists. After reviewing expert reports, he announced that Anthony was competent and the trial would continue.

Trial Winding Down ~ July 1, 2011
Defense has spent the last few days witnessing from various players, including the case of a meter leader who discovered Cary Anthony's body in December 2008. The final place to get rewards, the claims he denied in the stand.

The theory of the case raised by the defense includes the case where Casey Anthony was molested by her father, who lied about her feelings and the daughter for a month before her absence was reported. Hid the death of. However, they were struggling to prove this history because the only witness who tied Anthony to a molester was her fiance and his testimony was not authorized by Judge Perry. Even that witness only testified to Anthony, who claimed she was "groped" by her brother, and the defense never questioned her brother at the stand about the allegation.

The defense also questioned Cary's father, George Anthony, and brought out the attempted suicide he had made after Cary was discovered. This opened the door for the prosecution to bring in his suicide note as evidence during the counterargument, and that's exactly what they did. The reasons for attempting suicide did not include the accidental drowning of granddaughters as argued by the defense.

On June 30, the Casey Anthony trial defense abandoned the case, and on July 1, the prosecutor's office began a counterargument, expecting it to be completed by the end of the day. Perry declared that there was no court on July 2, and a deadline statement was issued on Sunday, July 3, allowing the jury to start deliberations before the holidays.

Closing Statement-2011
July 3, 2013 On July 3, Casey Anthony's state and defenders issued a closing statement, summarizing their claims before the jury began deliberations.

The state focused on Anthony's many lies throughout the time her daughter was missing, and then they discussed the items found on the body, claiming that no strangers could kill Cary. They argued that the defense theory of the case in which Cary died of accidental drowning hidden in her grandfather was illogical.

Defense lawmakers emphasized holes in the prosecution's suit, saying they didn't explain how Cayley died, lied to Anthony's side to a party, acted as a jury, and opposed her. Insisted. They dismissed the prosecution's allegations of Anthony's motives-she felt her daughter was in the way of the lifestyle she wanted.

When the statement was completed, the jury began deliberation.

Deliberation ~ 2011
July 5, 2014 On the morning of July 4, the jury of Casey Anthony trial began deliberation. On July 5, they will resume where

they left off six hours the day before.

Casey anthony
Pleaded guilty-July 5, 2011 After a 10-hour deliberation, a jury in Casey Anthony's trial ruled: acquitted of all major charges. They pleaded guilty to four causes of false information to the law enforcement agency in which she was charged, but acquitted of murder and child abuse charges.

Less than a week left in Casey Anthony's decision-July 7, 2011
After being accused of lying to law enforcement agencies, Casey Anthony was sentenced to four years by Jerry Perry, one year a year. Anthony has spent about three years in prison and behaved well, so Anthony will sentence in 13 weeks in a week. Perry fined Anthony $1,000 for each of the four counts.

DCF concludes Cary Anthony is responsible for Cary's death-August 12, 2011
While Casey Anthony was acquitted on trial for jury murder and child abuse, Florida's Children and Family Division reached another conclusion. They published a report saying Anthony was responsible for the death of her daughter. He does not claim to have done any physical harm to Cary, but has concluded that her child's inactivity for one month after being missing is not her best interest. This report is merely the conclusion of a departmental investigation and does not lead to further accusations against Anthony. Learn more about the story here.

Casey Anthony Probation-August 15, 2011
Casey Anthony's murder case judge Perry has issued another sentence on Anthony. This probation is for her belief in check fraud and has nothing to do with the murder trial that made her famous. Among other things, her probation prohibits drug and alcohol consumption, dealing with known criminals, and possession of firearms, and must be reported regularly to probation officers. The only difference in her probation from the standards of this type of crime is that Perry withholds her address for her protection. Since his innocence in July, Anthony has been called America's most hated person. During the probation period, the Corrections Department will do its best to protect her from the

angry mass.

Casey Anthony Fights Reimbursement Movement-September 2, 2011

As with Cayley's disappearance investigation, no one should be surprised that Casey Anthony's dramatic and very openly protracted trial paid Florida a fortune. Anthony was acquitted of the murder, but a jury convicted her of lying to the authorities about her daughter's disappearance, perhaps increasing the cost of the investigation (especially she later died after Kaley's death). I knew that I was out). On this basis, the prosecutor is moving to Anthony to cover these costs, which totals over $500,000. Her lawyer is fighting a move in court.

Casey Anthony costs almost $100,000 for research

Was ordered to repay ~ September 18, 2011 This may seem like a small expense to pay given the total cost of the survey. But the lawyer argued that this was a particularly unjustified amount to expect from her, as she was only charged four times for lying to police. Prosecutors argue that Anthony should be forced to repay these charges because the lie is "entangled" with the rest of the investigation.

Judge Belvin Perry said that under Florida law, Anthony could only charge the "reasonably necessary" cost to prove a conviction. This limit limits the charges for murder investigation or prosecution costs. The hearing decided that it was not possible to charge Anthony after 29 September 2008, which signaled the end of the missing person phase of the investigation.

Jerry Perry ordered Anthony to pay a total of $97,676.98.

$61,505.12 to Florida Law Enforcement Office
To Metropolitan Research Bureau 10,283.90
$25,837.96 to Orange County Sheriff's Office
$50.00 to the State Attorney's Office
Some of the Department of Security's expenses could not be disassembled to identify work performed prior to September 30, 2008. The judge instructed the investigators to file a revised report by September 18, 2011, and the total cost could be increased

accordingly. ..

Anthony Doubles and More Invoices-September 24, 2011

Casey Anthony's formal payment is $217,449.23, more than double the amount determined in the previous judgment but less than half the amount required by the state. This increase provided an additional $119,822.25 to the Sheriff's administrative expenses, following a series of new expense reports on the cost of the investigation.

Casey Anthony is still unemployed-2011

October 5, 2010 On Monday, October 3, Casey Anthony reported to a monthly meeting with her probation officer in Florida. She had no violations of probation conditions this month, according to a Florida DOC report. She reported that she had no work or income. The DOC report is here. Her probation conditions include finding a job, not taking illegal drugs, and reporting to a probation officer every month.

Casey Anthony Sues The Fifth – December 8, 2011

One of the lies Casey Anthony told earlier in her investigation into her daughter's disappearance, she was convicted in her criminal case, involving the nanny's name Zenaida Fernandez-Gonzalez. The nanny was revealed to be fictitious, but a woman named Zenaida Gonzalez subsequently claimed that Anthony's story brought extreme difficulties to her life, including the loss of work and apartments. As a result, she is suing Anthony for defamation. Anthony was sacked for civil action in October and used the fifth amendment (right to self-crime) 60 times to avoid answering questions. On December 8, 2011, a hearing was held to determine if she would be forced to answer these questions. The judge reserved the ruling on this matter. Please see here for the latest information on this.

Recent updates

Florida's Fifth District Court of Appeal throws two of four charges against the infamous mother, Casey Anthony, in accusing her of lying to police about the disappearance and death of her two-year-old daughter, Cary Anthony, in 2008. It was. The court, acquitted in the first murder of her daughter in 2011, sentenced her to four charges of "providing false information to law enforcement officers during an investigation of a missing person." .. She had already spent three years waiting for the trial.

However, the court accused two of these charges, arguing that they constituted a double risk. The double danger implies that you will be convicted twice for one crime and is not allowed by law. In addition, Anthony's lawyer argued that the four lies should be counted as a single crime. This was not accepted by the court, as there was enough time between the two lies to be a separate criminal offense. Anthony reserves the right to appeal the remaining two beliefs.

32 THE WALSH CHRONOLOGY

The son of John and Reve Walsh, Adam Walsh, was abducted on July 27, 1981, at the age of six. What was so scary about this story was what could have happened to anyone at the department store when I was absent for a little while at the fat. After searching the area, no one was able to find the missing child. Adam was killed. His amputated head was found two weeks later, but his body was never recovered.

A man named Otis Tur in Florida confessed to the murder in 1983, but was later withdrawn and not officially charged. Tool died in prison in 1996 while serving time for another murder he committed. However, in 2008 it was confirmed that he was a murderer and it was announced that the lawsuit had ended.

The reason for the long-standing litigation was due to procedural errors made in early 1981. Investigators lost some key evidence and were confused by the declined confession of tools. Still, police eventually realized that the circumstantial evidence was more than sufficient to convict Toole. Therefore, Adam's case was generally regarded as a failure of the judicial system, which spread new demands for higher quality police.

John Walsh began the television show America's Most Wanted in 1988 in grief, helping his parents to experience what he had experienced, as well as the Adam Walsh Children's Resource

Center and the Missing and Exploiting Children's Center. Established. The case also impacted the 2006 Adam Walsh Child Protection and Safety Act, establishing a more detailed and accessible national database of convicted sex offenders and criminal penalties for children. Raised and created a National Child Abuse Registration. The 2016 Adam Walsh Reauthorization Act continues to fund these efforts, and on October 7, 2016, the larger 2016 Survival Rights Act enacted several similar bills.

33 WHAT HAPPENED TO MEREDITH KERCHER?

Born July 9, 1987 in Seattle, Washington, Amanda Knox is best known for her conviction and acquittal in the 2007 murder of British roommate Meredith Karcher. At the time of the killing, the two college students lived together in Perugia, Italy. Knox was 20 and Kelcher was 21.

On the night of the murder, Knox spent the night with his boyfriend Rafaere Solesito. This caused suspicion among investigators. The first authorities to arrive at the scene were the postal police. Don't kill a field agent who has been found to be one of the many flaws in the investigation. They will find Karcher's dead body on the floor of her bedroom, covered with a bloody duvet. The cause of death was suffocation and blood loss due to a knife injury.

Knox and Sollecito were brought in to interrogate the site that was interrogated for five days. Knox later claimed that he had no interpreter and was bullied and beaten while she was in police custody. Knox confessed that she was in the next room while Kercher was murdered by her current boss, Patrick Lumumba.

In November 2007, Italian police announced that Karcher's murderer was confirmed and both Knox and Solesito were arrested. Lumumba's alibi was that he was working on the night of the murder. Two weeks later, forensic evidence found on the scene pointed to Rudigede, a friend of an Italian man who lived in an apartment under two girls. He admitted to being on the scene, but denied any other involvement. The following year, Gede was convicted and sentenced to 30 years in prison.

Knox and Solicito chose to be tested together. They were convicted of 26 and 25 years respectively. The prosecution portrayed Knox as sexually crazy "her devil." They also created an elaborate scene where Karcher was an unlucky victim of a sex game and was misorganized by Knox. The lawsuit became a media circus and Knox supporters claimed that she was being discriminated against because she was an attractive American woman. The effectiveness of the Italian legal system was also scrutinized.

The decision did not end there. In October 2011 Sollecito and Knox were acquitted on murder charges. Shortly after returning home in 2013, both Knox and Soleshto were ordered to try again for the killing of the later guilty Karcher.

In March 2015, the Italian Supreme Court overturned the 2014 conviction for "clear errors."

34 THE ANDREA YATES CASE: INSANITY ON TRIAL

Andrea Yeats (born Andrea Kennedy) was born in Houston, Texas in 1964. Since 1999, she has been suffering from depression and psychosis, but was generally happy with her husband Rusty Yates. Together, they had five children.

The birth of her fifth child and the death of her father brought something new to her and her depression was exacerbated. In 2001, after a stint on the treatment network, she was prescribed the antipsychotic drug Haldol. Her psychiatrist, Mohammed Saeed, decided that later in the year Haldol was no longer needed and took her out of medicine.

Just 16 days later, Rusty Yates on duty received a horrifyingly disturbing phone call from his wife. She briefly said to him, "I did it." He returned home and discovered that his wife drowned five children in a bathtub.

During her trial, Yates' defense was crazy. Nevertheless, she was sentenced to death in prison. However, there was a retrial in 2006 after it was discovered that one psychiatrist, Park Dietz, gave testimony that proved to be untrue. He claimed that Yates got her idea of drowning children from an episode of law and order. It turns out he confused the plans for multiple episodes. Upon receiving this information, Yates was handed a new sentence: acquitted for madness. She and her husband divorced. He currently lives in Kerrville State Hospital indefinitely.

35 THE BLACK DAHLIA MURDER

On January 15, 1947, Elizabeth Short's body was discovered at Lymart Park in Los Angeles, California. A woman walks in the park with her two-year-old daughter after seeing what she thought was an abandoned mannequin. She quickly realized that the corpse was a corpse and grabbed the daughter running to the nearest phone to call the police.

Elizabeth Short's body was cut in half at her waist and her blood was drained. Her face was clipped from her mouth to her ears, giving her what people nowadays call the "joker's smile." Her skin and thigh had numerous cuts and bruises as part of her skin was removed. An autopsy showed she was eventually killed due to laceration and bleeding on her head due to a blow to her face.

After making the LAPD claiming that nearly 50 men and women where it happened were murderers, this made it very difficult for police to identify the killer. There were numerous suspects throughout the year, but there was not enough evidence to prosecute anyone. There were multiple theories of murder and how they could be related to other murders. Some detectives believed that the same person who committed the Cleveland torso murderer also killed Elizabeth Short. Another feasible theory at one time was that Mr. Short's murder was associated with the murder of lipstick. Many believe that the main reason for the unsolved murder case was due to media interference in the investigation. Cops and detectives said reporters had examined the evidence and withheld the information they received from calling offices. At some point, the reporters were at the LAPD station, free to answer calls that might have withheld information that could help them investigate.

Elizabeth Short received the name "Black Dahlia" as the script for the popular movie "Blu-Dahlia" at the time. This name was created and generalized by media and news reporters. The main misconception caused by many writers at the time was that she was a call girl, but there was no evidence of that.

The Black Dahlia murder case is one of the most famous unsolved murder cases in the world. The gruesome nature of the crime helped to strengthen its bad reputation. New evidence has been discovered over the years, but many believe it is an unsolved murder.

36 CHARLES MANSON AND THE MANSON FAMILY

The terrifying crimes committed by the Manson and the Mansons are:

Get acquainted with the prominent members of the Mansons:
Charles Manson-Leader of the Manson family, operational mastermind behind a series of murders
Charles "Tex" Watson
Beausoleil
Mary Brunner
Susan Atkins
Linda Casabian
Patricia Crenwinkel
Leslie Van Gauteng
Steve Grogan

Notable victims:
Gary Hinman-Manson family friend and victim of the killings
Sharon Tate-actress, pregnant murder victim
Roman Polanski-Sharon Tate's husband who was not at home at the time
Abigail Volger-Heir to Volger Coffee Fortune, murder victim
Woichev Frikovsky-writer, lover of Folger, victim of murder

Jason Sebring – Hair Stylist, Sharon Tate's Best Friend, Victim of the Killing

Lenora Bianca – Founder of State Wholesale Grocery Company, Killer Victim

Rosemary La Bianca-Boutique Carriage Co-Founder, Lenora Bianca's Wife, Victim of Murder

Bernard Crowe – Manson Barbara Hoyt scam victim

– Former family prosecution witness, the Manson family

Attempt to Kill Dennis Wilson – Beach Boys Member, Former Manson Friend

Hinman killing

Charles "Tex" Watson tricked Bernard Crow into winning Manson's money. Crow threatened Manson and the Mansons. Shortly thereafter, Manson falsely pretended Crow to be part of the Black Panthers, an African-American leftist organization. However, Claw did not die and Manson feared retaliation from him. Manson needed money to escape and move to a new area away from the Sparn Ranch (Mansons estate). During Manson's escape plan, it was said that his friend Gary Hinman was making some money from heritage.

Manson, along with Mary Brunner and Susan Atkins, ordered Bobby Beausoleil to persuade him to go to Hinman's residence and return the money in order to recover it from Hinman. Hinman was not supportive. After being held hostage for several days, Manson came with a sword and cut Hinman's left ear. Eventually, Beausoleil stabbed Hinman twice in his chest and killed him. Hinman blood was used to smear a "political piggy bank" on the wall, along with Black Panther's legs, to involve the Black Panther Party.

There is a lot of speculation about the circumstances surrounding the murder of Hinman, but Beausoleil was arrested because he slept in Hinman's car and wore bloody clothes when he was stabbed, and his murder weapon was hidden in the tires of his trunk. It was.

Tate Murder

Actress Sharon Tate and director Roman Polanski rented a

house together in a semi-isolated location in the Beverly Hills canyon of Cielo Drive. On August 9, 1969, pregnant Tate was having fun with her friend when her unborn baby, Polanski's father and lover were not there. The nights with Tate were Abigail Folger, Vojchev-Flikowski, and Jay Sebring.

Later in the night, Tate's neighbor claimed to have heard of the shooting, but did not warn authorities. There were also reports of a man screaming from the Tate House. Late in the evening, private security officers hired by the property owner also heard gunfire from the Tate House and began notifying the Los Angeles Police Department (LAPD).

At 8am the next morning, the housekeeper Winifred Chapman entered the dwelling and found the body brutally killed.

According to the book Helter Skelter-The true story of the Manson murder, by Vincent Baggliosi (eg lead prosecutor) and Kurt Gentry, Charles Manson enters Tate's residence with Charles Watson, Susan Atkins, Linda Casabian, and so on. Directed Patricia Crenwinkel (formerly Melson's House, who refused to edit Mason's music) and "destroy everyone in it-as terrifying as possible". Watson, Atkins, Kasabian and Crenwinkel all climbed to a raised platform to get to the hotel entrance. While they were trespassing, Stephen Parent, a visitor to the residence caretaker William Garretson, was leaving property in the car. Watson stopped his parent, shook the knife at him, and shot four times in his chest and abdomen.

Watson cut the window screen into the dwelling and opened the front doors of Atkins and Clenwinkel. Kasabian was at the end of the driveway, "keeping watch." Watson and the group entered the dwelling and found Tate, Folger, Frikovsky, and Sebring. Tate and Sebring were tied at their necks and Folger was taken to a nearby bedroom. Sebring was shot and stabbed seven times. Frikovow was tied up with a towel, but managed to free himself. After doing so, he was involved in a physical relationship with Atkins, and she stuck him in his leg. Frikovsky continued to run away, but Watson repeatedly hit him with a gun over his head, shooting and stabbing him several times. Watson's overhead attack on Frikovsky resulted in broken gun grip.

Folger escaped from the room he was taken to and was chased by Krenwinkel. Folger was stabbed by Cren Winkel and eventually Watson. Folger was stabbed a total of 28 times by both Crenwinkel and Watson. Meanwhile, Frikowski was struggling across the lawn when Watson again stabbed him. Frikovsky was stabbed 51 times in total.

Witnessing a horrific crime, Tate appealed to Atkins for mercy but was denied. Tate was stabbed 16 times in total. Tate's fetus did not survive the event.

Labianca murder
On August 10, 1969, the night after the Tate murder, Manson and the six Manson family (Leslie Van Gouten, Steve Grogan, Susan Atkins, Linda Casabian, Patricia Crenwinkel, Charles Watson) committed another murder. Unlike the Tate murder, Manson participated in the Labianca murder. Because he felt there was not enough panic among the victims of the Tate killing. Manson and his family drove a car in search of a potential murder victim when they arrived in the neighborhood of a house that was attending a party a year ago. The house next door was owned by the owner of a successful grocery company, Lenora Bianca and his wife, Rosemary.

The exact event of the murder is uncertain, as there are several different accounts from Manson and the six Manson family. Manson claims he approached the house alone and later returned to bring Watson. When Manson and Watson were in their place of residence, they tied the Rabianka couple with a cord of lamps and a pillow cover over their heads. Manson reassured that he had been robbed because he would not hurt the couple. All the cash was collected and the bordered rosemary was returned to her room. Shortly thereafter, Van Houten and Kren Winkel entered the grounds with instructions from Manson to kill the couple. Manson left the mansion and instructed Van Houten and Cren Winkel to follow Watson's orders.

When Watson yelled to stop sticking Reno, Watson began to

stick Reno many times. Then, in the bedroom, Rosemary began to shake the lamp, still attached to the cord wrapped around his neck. Van Gauteng and Cren Winkel shouted for Watson's help and stabbed Rosemary over and over. Watson handed the knife to Van Houten and she continued to stab the rosemary. Rosemary was stabbed a total of 41 times by Watson, Van Houten, and Kren Winkel.

Watson returned to the living room, stabbed Reno and continued to kill him. Krenwinkel carved the word "WAR" into Reno's stomach, pierced Reno several times, pushed a carving fork out of his stomach, and left a knife in Reno's throat. Reno was stabbed a total of 26 times.

On the wall of the living room, "Pig's death" and "Rise" were written in Reno's blood. The refrigerator door was painted with a misspelled "Healter [sic] Skelter".

Rosemary's son, Frank Strussers, from a previous marriage was suspected of being shaded after returning from a campaign trip. He also suspected that Reno's speedboat was still parked on the driveway. The Strothers called on his sister to warn her, and she came with her boyfriend, Joe Dogan. Dogan and The Strassers enter the house through the side door and discover Reno's body. A warning has been issued to LAPD.

Investigation
As mentioned above, Tate's housekeeper discovered the body the morning after the murder and called for a LAPD investigator. The Hinman killing is under the jurisdiction of the Los Angeles Security Office (LASD), and Beausoleil has been arrested. The La Bianca murder case was under the jurisdiction of LAPD, but a formal announcement by LAPD falsely confirmed that the Tate and La Bianca murder cases were not related.

The Tate murder investigation was initially arrested for finding housekeeper Garretson on the scene. He was released after passing the polygraph test.

While LASD contacted LAPD for the striking similarities

between the Tate and Hinman killings, LAPD claimed that the Tate killing was the result of a drug trade.

There was lack of inter-agency communication at the beginning of each survey. This led to another dead end to the murder investigation. Fortunately, continued criminal activity within the Mansons helped police authorities arrest more than 12 individuals. While the Mansons were digging "bottomless holes" in Death Valley, they burned machines belonging to Death Valley National Monument. When they burned the machine, police stormed the Death Valley ranch. During the raid, police found multiple stolen vehicles and conducted multiple arrests. Beausoleil's girlfriend, Kittilte Singer, was arrested on the ranch with the Mansons. When the detective of Rabyanka discovered Lute Singer's relationship with Beausoleil, the detective of Rabyanka spoke to her. She informed Labianca's detective that Manson was looking for a bodyguard from a motorcycle gang on Span Ranch. In addition, she informed the detective that Atkins was involved in the Hintmann murder, as Lutechinger's boyfriend Beausoleil was arrested. Meanwhile, Atkins began sharing details of the Tate murder with her two-tier mate in prison, admitting he was involved in the Hinman murder. These details will quickly launch a murder investigation into the Tate murder, further linking the Manson family to the Labianca murder. Atkins began sharing details of the Tate murder with her bunks in prison and admitted he was involved in the Hinman murder. These details will quickly launch a murder investigation of the Tate murder, further linking the Manson family to the Labianca murder. Atkins began sharing details of the Tate murder with her bunks in prison and admitted he was involved in the Hinman murder. These details will quickly launch a murder investigation of the Tate murder, further linking the Manson family to the Labianca murder.

Physical evidence was collected for Watson and Crenwinkel, including fingerprints. In addition, a unique .22 Koehler Hi Standard revolver with broken grip was found in a property near Tate House. Property owner Bernard Weiss turned the weapon into a LAPD a few months before breaking new research. Reading the incident and broken grip details at the Los Angeles Times, Weiss contacted LAPD about the weapons found in the backyard.

LAPD discovered the weapon as evidence and linked the gun to the Tate murder.

The LAPD issued arrest warrants for Watson, Kasabian, and Crenwinkel involved in the killing of Tate, and also in the killing of Labianka. Watson and Crenwinkel were arrested in various states, and Kasabian voluntarily surrendered when he discovered a warrant for arrest. No warrants were made because Manson and Atkins were already in custody for unrelated crimes on Death Valley ranches.

Approaching
The motivational Manson philosophy of the coming Apocalypse was the true motive behind the murder. He told his family that the "Helter Skelter" was coming. According to Manson, Herter Skelter was the uprising of the racial war between "blackish" and "whiteish". Until the end of the "war," he hid himself and his family in a cave in Death Valley to benefit from racial warfare. He promotes this war by killing "white men" and engaging the African-American community in a variety of ways, including disposing of victims' wallets in areas where African-American residents are very high. ..

trial
On June 15, 1970, the Tate Labianca trial against Manson, Watson, Atkins, and Klukinkel began with seven murders and one conspiracy case. Van Houten was charged with two murders and one conspiracy. In exchange for immunity, Kasabian gave testimony from the prosecution to explain what happened during each malicious crime. Atkins originally agreed to testify, but withdrew her statement. At the beginning of the trial, Manson was allowed by the court to act as his own lawyer. However, after some behavior violations, the permission to represent him was revoked. As a result, Manson marked an "X" on his forehead in opposition to the withdrawn permit.

After a month of tragic events, a jury was elected. Linda Casabian was called to the stand by Bugliosis after disagreeing that Canalek was incompetent and insane. The opposition was dismissed and Kasabian was sworn as a witness. She was on stand for a total of 18 days, seven of which were for cross-examination. Manson confused Casabian's testimony by revealing the newspaper headline "Manson Guilty, Nixon Declaration." Defense lawyers used this to create prejudice for scandals. The request was denied because the jury swore to the judge that he was not affected by the presidential declaration.

Manson's influence on the prosecution's witnesses was becoming apparent during the trial. For example, prosecution Witness Barbara Hoyt was invited to Hawaii by a Mansons family and was given a lethal LSD. Fortunately, Hoyt was able to reach the hospital before the fatal event happened. Another witness who was threatened was Paul Watkins. Watkins was badly burned by a suspicious fire in his van.

In addition, Van Houten's lawyer Ronald Hughes was unable to appear in court because he refused to testify of the client. He said he refused to "push the client out of the window." Hughes' body was discovered after the trial and his death is rumored to have been ordered by the Mansons.

Disturbance
Manson actively expressed his views and opinions regarding the testimony and statements made by the prosecution. A memorable moment happened when Manson and the judge fell into disagreement and Manson threw himself at the judge and shouted, "Someone should cut off your head." Shortly thereafter, the women of the Mansons began chanting Latin chants in favor of the Manson explosion.

Prosecutors ended the case and turned their attention to the defense team. To everyone's surprise, the defense declared that their case was absent. As a result, the woman began protesting to testify and all the lawyers were summoned to the Chamber of Commerce. The defense team strongly opposed the client's testimony, as they felt that the woman was still under Manson's influence and were the only perpetrators involved in the crime. Judge Alder declared that the right to testify takes precedence over attorney objections. When Atkins disagreed with the testimony, the lawyer refused to ask her questions. Manson stood on the stand the next day and witnessed the incident for over an hour. During this time, the jury was exempted to prevent evidence that barred co-defendants from prejudicing the jury.

Watson was tried in August 1971 and convicted of seven murder cases and one conspiracy case.

verdict

The jury spent a week deliberating and found guilty of all charges of murder and conspiracy against all defendants. During the trial, the jury declared the death penalty. Following the California Supreme Court's ruling in 1972, the death penalty for all defendants was put in prison.

Current…

Manson was in prison in Corcoran, California. He was denied parole each time the hearing was held, for a total of 12 times. On January 1, 2017, Manson was taken to a hospital and found to be suffering from gastrointestinal bleeding. Though still very ill, he was returned to prison. He was taken back to the hospital on November 15th of that year. Just four days later, while still in the hospital, Manson died of cardiac arrest due to respiratory failure and colon cancer. He was 83 years old.

Susan Atkins served life imprisonment at the Central California Women's Facility in Chowchilla, California until her death on September 24, 2009. She was 61 years old.

Patricia Crenwinkel is a life imprisonment student at the California Girls Academy in Chino, California. In 2017 she was denied parole 14 times.

Leslie Van Gauteng currently works for the California Women's Education Institution in Frontera, California. As of 2018, she has been denied a total of 21 paroles.

Charles "Tex" Watson is currently serving life imprisonment at the Richard J. Donovan Correctional Facility in San Diego, California.

Bobby Beausoleil began his prison sentence for more than 30 years in 1970. He is currently housed in the California Medical Facility in Vacaville, California.

Steve Grogan was released on parole in 1985.

Linda Casavian was dismissed from California after the trial, given the immunity of being a key witness to the prosecution.

Tate's mansion was demolished and a new mansion was built on site. The house remains vacant. The La Bianca House is a private residence and was launched for sale in 2019.

37 CHRISTIAN LONGO: FAMILY ANNIHILATOR

At first glance, Christian Longo looked like a charming and charming family. Friends, family, and the entire country were amazed when he turned out to be a cold-blooded hitman. In the late 1990s, life with Christian Longo's wife Mary Jane and her three children Zachary, Saddy, and Madison seemed perfect from the outside. But a few days before Christmas 2001, this perfect family was destroyed.

On December 19, 2001, the body of 4-year-old Zachary Longo was found floating in a marina in Waldport, Oregon. Shortly thereafter, the body of Sadilongo was also discovered. Eight days later, the worst fears of the country were realized when the bodies and bodies of Mary Jane and Madison Longo were found to be packed in a suitcase floating near a Longo apartment in the Bay of Yaquina. After each body was discovered, investigators put Christian Longo, the family's only missing person, on the FBI's 10 Most Wanted Lists. Longo fled, but was not found anywhere, and the FBI continued to investigate why his seemingly perfect husband had killed the entire family.

Research has shown that Longo has been involved in criminal activity for some time. After leaving the New York Times distributor, Longo tried to launch his own company, which became a financial disaster. As his debt increased, Longo began making counterfeit checks from customer checks. Despite his rogue way of making money, he bought expensive cars and had a luxurious vacation. Longo's easy-going method ended when he was charged with making a counterfeit check. He was sentenced to probation and light indemnity, but his life changed dramatically. Longo was found cheating on his wife and was expelled from his church for a long list of misconduct. He wanted to start a better life and took his family from his Michigan home to a warehouse in Toledo, Ohio.

On the day Mary Jane and Madison Longo were discovered, it was discovered that Christian Longo was using a stolen identity from former New York Times author Michael Finkel to board a flight to Cancun, Mexico. After Longo was identified by American tourists, Mexican authorities handed him over to the United States.

Longo claims in an official trial that his wife Mary Jane killed her two oldest children and was angry at murdering Mary Jane and his youngest child, raged by poor financial conditions Did. Within four hours, the jury was convicted and Christian Longo was sentenced to death by a lethal injection.

Shortly after the trial, Christian Longo initiated the appeals process, which is estimated to last 5 to 10 years. In 2011, Longo was sentenced to death in Oregon after acknowledging his family's murder.

In popular culture:
While Longo was awaiting trial, he visited Michael Finkel, a man who claims to be himself in Mexico. Then a strange friendship was born. As before, Longo captivated Finkel, expecting him to be innocent. Their friendship worsened when Longo ran for trial. Finkel wrote a memoir in 2005 entitled "True Story: Murder, Memoir, Mea Culpa" about his relationship with Longo. In 2015, it became the movie "True Story" starring James Franco as Longo and Jonahill as Finkel.

38 THE MANHUNT FOR CHRISTOPHER DORNER

On February 3, 2013, a former LAPD officer named Christopher Donner attacked and killed Monica Quan and his fiancee Key Lawrence. The incident triggered a nine-day search for Donor to commit suicide.

Christopher Donner was born in New York on June 4, 1979. He spent his childhood in Los Angeles, transferring between schools in the area. After graduating from University of Southern Utah in 2001, Dorner joined the Navy Reserve. On February 1, 2013, two days before he committed multiple murders, he was honored as a lieutenant officer from the Navy.

While Christopher Donner was in the Navy Reserve, he joined the Los Angeles Police Department in 2005 and completed training in 2006. A year later, in 2007, Donner submitted a report to the trainer Teresa Evans for using excessive force against a mentally ill man. Who did they arrest? Donner alleged that Evans kicked the arrested person while handcuffed while standing on the ground. His claim was rejected because it could not be substantiated. Donor was dismissed from LAPD in 2008. He has appealed his case multiple times, but courts upheld the LAPD decision. Donner argued that his racist colleagues worked to erode his credit and end his career. His final appeal was dismissed in late 2011.

On February 3, 2013, Donna approached Monica Quan, 28, and her fiance, Keys Lawrence, 27, at 27. Monica Kuan's father was Randal Kuan, the LAPD captain who had acted as Donor at the hearing. Donor posted on Facebook to warn Randal Kuang of the impact of Donor's dismissal on him and his family. A Facebook post has made Donner a leading suspect in the murder case.

During the search, Donner won a loyal fan on social media. Prodorner hashtags like #WeStandWithDorner are popular all over the world.

On February 12, 2013, nine days after running, Donner was taken hostage in a cabin at Big Bear Lake, California. Then he left the house in the stolen car. My wife managed to get free and warned the police. After Donner left the cabin, he encountered and shot a marked police car driven by a game watchman. The San Bernardino County Sheriff's Office surrounded the rural area of Christopher Dorner. Two police officers were injured and one was killed during the subsequent shootout. Christopher evacuated to a hut in the mountains, where he continued firing at police. The cabin exploded suddenly, and police believe this was due to the smoke bomb they were using to pull out Donner. Police have found that his charcoal remains in the cabin. Autopsy showed that he was killed by a bullet that fired spontaneously.

The $1 million reward for the information that led to Donner's capture was distributed to four people.

39 WHAT HAPPENED TO DREW PETERSON?

Drew Peterson is a former police officer from Bolingbrook, Illinois. After graduating high school and marrying his first wife, Carroll Brown, Peterson joined the army. After two years of service, he joined the police station. After serving as a patrol officer, he was promoted to a drug unit where he worked as an undercover agent.

When Peterson learned that he had a secret flirt, his first wife filed for divorce. Apart from two engagements, he gets married three more times. He married his second wife, Victoria Connolly, in 1982. Connolly later discusses how Peterson was abusive and dominant not only to her, but to her daughter of a previous marriage. Peterson was also under investigation by his police unit for not reporting bribery or misconduct during the infiltration, for which he was temporarily fired and then demoted. This put additional stress on the relationship. Peterson began an affair with his third wife, Catherine Savio, while still married to Connolly. Peterson and Savio were married two months after the divorce between Peterson and Connolly was confirmed in 1992. In 2002 Savio received a protection order against Peterson due to domestic violence. Savio was suppressed by Peterson's rule and withdrew from friends and family throughout the relationship. Peterson was also watching his future fourth wife, Stacy, during marriage. The couple's divorce was completed in 2003. Between 2002 and 2004, there were reports of 18 domestic disturbances at Peterson's home, with the notation that it had been abusing, destroying, invading Peterson, and delaying the children of the pair from visiting. did.

The last weekend of February 2004 was one of the weekends Peterson spent with the children of Savio. That Sunday, he went to his ex-wife's house and returned the children, but no one answered the door or phone. By Monday, March 1, there were no signs of Savio yet. Peterson asked some neighbors to enter the house with him, where they found Savio in the bathtub. The bathtub was dry while her hair was damp. There was a rip in her head and she was unresponsive. Initial physical and hearing tests declared death as an accident, but those who knew Savio were already suspicious of Peterson.

His alibi against Savio's death was his fourth wife, Stacy. A thirty-year-old junior Stacy suffered from the limited nature of his relationship with Peterson. In October 2007, Stacy was supposed to help her sister's painting, but she didn't show up. Her older sister filed a report of the missing person on October 29. Peterson said officials said the wife had left him for another man, while many who knew her had said she would not abandon her child. No trace of her has ever been found.

Not surprisingly, media and police generally renewed interest in Peterson's third wife's death, as suspicion naturally fell to Peterson with the disappearance of his fourth wife. Savio's death was ruled as a murder because a doctor unfamiliar with Peterson dug up his body and examined it. In 2009, Peterson was charged with killing Savio. The majority of the lawsuits relied on "hiassay" evidence, which is usually not permitted, but the Illinois state legislature passed "Drew's Law" in 2008 for an exception, hearing some of the evidence. I was able to. In September 2012, Peterson was convicted. Peterson has served 38 years in prison for Savio's death. On May 31, 2016, Peterson was sentenced to another 40 years after he was convicted of attempting to attack James Glasgow, a state lawyer in Will County.

40 WHY THE MENENDEZ BROTHERS KILLED THEIR PARENTS?

Two brothers, Eric and Lyle Menendez, raised in Beverly Hills, California, were convicted of murdering their parents, Jose and Louise "Kitty" Menendez, on the night of August 20, 1989.

The boy's father, Jose Menendez, emigrated from Cuba at the age of 16 to work in corporate America, become a very wealthy businessman, and eventually become the CEO of LIVE Entertainment.

At ages 21 and 18, Lyle and Eric planned to kill his father, and his mother bought a shotgun a few days before the murder. Prosecutors argued that the blessed brothers killed their parents from greed in hopes of acquiring their family's property early.

On the night of August 20, 1989, Eric and Lyle Menendez fired at Jose and Kitty in the Beverly Hills Mansion. Lyle shot his father several times in his arms and once in his head with a Mossberg 12-gauge shotgun. Kitty was shot on her torso and face and she is unrecognizable. They kneel and shoot both Kitty and Jose to make the case look like a mob hit.

Lyle and Eric picked up all the shells, drove the Mulholland Drive and threw a shotgun into the canyon. They returned home and called the police. When the police arrived, Eric and Lyle ran outside the play's display and shouted so.

Les Zoeller was assigned to the case and when he examined the crime scene, he found that there was no forced intrusion and it did not look like a robbery. However, Zorer did not consider the brothers suspects and did not conduct a gunshot residue inspection. During the question, Eric was very emotionally unstable, but Lyle was calmly collected. When asked if someone wanted to kill his parents, Lyle replied "maybe a mob." The coroner determined that the shot to her left knee came from a different angle than the other shots, so the killer may have staged the murder and looked like a mob job.

Eric was young and frail and suffered much more psychologically than Lyle. He confessed the killing to his psychiatrist Dr. Jerome Ogiel and immediately reported his confession to Lyle. Lyle confronted Ogiel and threatened his life. Instead of calling the police, Ogiel returned to his brothers several times to tape the session, but kept the confession secret.

Meanwhile, the brothers spent extravagance after their parents died. The detective linked the two brothers to the murder and began looking for physical evidence. Investigator Zoller tracked the sale of two Mossberg shotguns on August 18, 1990, two days before the murder occurred. The man listed as a customer proved he was working in New York during the murder and pointed out that the signature wasn't close to him. Zoller saw the opportunity and demanded that Eric and Lyle take a handwritten test, but Eric refused.

In March 1990, Dr. Ogiel's mistress, angry that she had just broken up, went to police and told them that the Menendez brothers had confessed to see Ogiel for psychiatry and murder his parents. It was. On March 8, 1990, Lyle Menendez was arrested while having lunch with a friend. Eric Menendez, who traveled to Israel, learned of his arrest and soon set out.

There was controversy over whether the tape that Ojiel made with his brothers' confession was subject to the patient therapist's confidentiality laws. When Eric threatened Ogier's life, the patient doctor's confidentiality was finally ruled to have been breached, and some of the tape is considered acceptable evidence.

During the first trial, Menendez lawyers began defending Eric and Lyle as victims of child abuse by their father when they were very young. In the course of the trial, defense defenders violently attacked the personalities of both Jose and Kitty, showing that the brothers felt "imminent danger." Neither brother had told the psychiatrist, friends, or family anything like that, so the prosecution could easily break the claim. Both juries announced that they were unable to reach a decision due to a deadlock, and both cases were tort.

The second trial was deliberately under-published and unpublished because the judge felt that the jury in the first trial was affected by media coverage of the case. On April 17, 1996, a jury decided that life in prison without the possibility of parole was the highest punishment for the brothers. They have been sentenced to another institution and have not been in contact for years since then, but have been contacted in writing.

Eric Menendez is currently at the Richard J. Donovan Correctional Facility and Lyle Menendez is at Mule Creek State Jail. Both of them are married and sentenced to life imprisonment without the possibility of parole because they have no children.

41 GOLDEN STATE KILLER

The Golden State Killer is one of the most notorious serial killer in US history. Golden State Killer, also known as the Visalia Run Soccer, East Area Reapist, and Original Nightstalker, operated from Sacramento to Santa Barbara county from 1974 to 1986, with at least 13 murders, more than 50 rapes, and 100 people. The robber who did the above rape. In 2013, the true criminal writer Michelle McNamara created the name Golden State Killer to cover the various monikers given to criminals.

Visalia Run Soccer
In 1974, Visalia was a small town halfway between Sacramento and Los Angeles and was the center of a series of over 100 robbers. Robbers roamed around the homeowner's belongings, mostly removing low-priced items, coins, and women's underwear. In September 1975, a man who was strongly believed to be run football invaded Claude Snelling's house in an attempt to kidnap Snelling's daughter. The intruder shot Snelling twice and escaped because Snelling died of an injury. Although another invasion and shooting attempt was made in December of that year, Run Soccer again evaded police. The robbers stopped in Visalia after the December attack.

Eastern part
Rape Crime In June 1976, the East Sacramento area became a hunting ground for continuous rape criminals. The criminal

creeped up on a woman in the area and began to peep through the window. On June 18, 1976, he invaded a single woman's house in Rancho Cordova and escalated to a rape raped at Knife Point. He committed at least 49 rapes in the East Sacramento area and surrounding cities. The last rape was Danville, just outside San Francisco, on June 11, 1979. In 1978, the Eastern rapist killed Katie and Brian Maggiore during a dog walk in Rancho Cordova.

Original night stalker

On October 1, 1979, he invaded a house in Southern California town of Goleta and tied up a couple living there. Fortunately, the neighbors heard the couple cry and called the police. He fled the scene by bicycle. He was called the Night Stalker, but was renamed the original Night Stalker after Richard Ramirez received the same moniker. Original Night Stalker murdered four more couples and a woman in Southern California between 1979 and 1981, and raped them before killing them. The murder stopped until 1986 and raped and killed 18-year-old Janer Cruz.

Joseph De Angelo

After the killing of Janel Cruz in 1986, no more crimes were attributed to the Eastern Rape or the original night stalker. At that time, it was believed that the two crime sprees were related, but in some cases DNA proof that the rapes of the East and the original night stalker were the same, though not officially connected until 2001. I proved to be a person. Following contact in 2001, the lawsuit remained silent until 2016, when authorities announced new efforts to capture elusive criminals. On April 24, 2018, Joseph James DeAngelo was arrested and charged with eight first-degree murder charges in connection with the original Night Stalker case. It was revealed that he was strongly suspected of the Viseria Run football case. In August, DeAngelo was charged with 13 abductions/abductions in connection with the Eastern Region rapist case. He was not charged with rape because the restrictions passed.

Joseph De Angelo was 72 when he was arrested. From 1973 to 1976, De Angelo was a police officer in Exeter, a small town not far from Visalia. In 1976, I joined police in Auburn, about 30 minutes drive from Sacramento. He was dismissed from the job in

1979 when he caught a hammer from a shoplifting dog water repellent and a local convenience store. He moved to Citrus Heights in 1980 and lived there until he was arrested.

DeAngelo was identified through GEDmatch, a free DNA sharing site that allows individuals to upload their DNA profiles from services such as 23andMe and MyHeritage. In 2018, police uploaded a DNA sample of a 1978 crime related to the Golden State Killer. DNA reduced nearly one million profiles to one family, and with the help of other factors such as approximate age and geographical proximity, authorities were able to narrow down one suspect. After De Angelo was confirmed on April 19, 2018, he was put under police supervision. Police were able to collect a DNA sample from the door handle of his car and collect discarded tissue that matched the DNA collected at the crime scene associated with the Golden State Killer.

Using a DNA database to finally figure out the Golden State Killer is very controversial. Family DNA has been used by national authorities to identify and capture suspected heinous crimes, but those who believe that the ability of the government to search criminal DNA databases is a violation of privacy. I also have People who have never uploaded a DNA sample can be identified through distant families, as in DeAngelo. According to a study published in Science Magazine, about 60% of European descent and about 40% of sub-Saharan African descent in the United States can be identified using the MyHeritage DNA database alone.

42 THE MYSTERIOUS MURDER OF TRAVIS ALEXANDER

Jodialias met Travis Alexander at a business meeting in Las Vegas, Nevada in September 2006. The two soon became friends, and in November of the same year, Arias was baptized by the Mormon Faith, the Church of Alexander. A few months later, the two were dating, but in the summer of 2007, they broke up and Alexander began dating another woman. Around the same time, Alexander told a friend he believed Arias was stalking him, but the two continued a fragmented friendship. They continued to communicate when Aria moved to California.

Travis Alexander was killed at his home in Mesa, Arizona on June 4, 2008. He made 27 stings, a slit throat, and a gunshot on his face. Alexander intended to go on a trip to Cancun, Mexico on June 10. Initially, he was planning to take her girlfriend, Jodialias, on a trip, but reportedly decided to take another woman, Mimihall, in April instead. ..

After Alexander was absent from the conference call, worried friends entered his house and in the shower found a pool of blood leading to his body. The 911 phone involved Arias as a former girlfriend who was stalking Alexander. The house of her grandparents in Arias, California, where she lived was robbed in May 2008. The prosecution speculated that Arias had robbed himself and used the gun he stole to kill Alexander. In the time between Alexander's death on June 4th and the discovery of his body on June 9, Arias repeatedly left a message on his voicemail. She did this to keep her away from the crime scene and appear to worry about Alexander's health.

At the crime scene, investigators found Alexander's damaged digital camera. They were finally able to recover an image containing a time stamped sexually provocative pose Arias and Alexander at about 1:40 pm on June 4, 2008. The last picture of Alexander Alive was taken at 5:29 pm in the shower, and shortly after that, an accidental image of a possibly bleeding person, perhaps Alexander. The investigators used the time stamps on the photos to determine the exact time of death of Alexander. The investigators found a bloody palm pattern in the corridor. This was a mixture of Alexander and Arias DNA.

During the investigation, Arias claimed that she last saw Alexander in April 2008, despite the photographs and evidence of DNA that left her home on the day of the killing. Later, she changed her story and said she was at home when two intruders invaded and attacked both, eventually killing Alexander.

Arias was charged with first-class murder on July 9, 2008, and acquitted on September 11, 2008. The trial began in January 2013. The prosecution has charged Arias for the death penalty. On February 6, Arias testified that he had killed Alexander for self-defense and said he had been abusive during their relationship. On May 8, 2013, the jury reached a verdict. Jodi Arias was convicted of the first murder. The juries did not reach agreement on whether the murder was planned.

Arias' strange behavior during the study prompted experts to diagnose her with post-traumatic stress disorder and borderline personality disorder.

On May 16, the trial period began. The jury will have to decide whether Arias will be sentenced to death or living in prison. On May 21, Arias granted life imprisonment in spite of being added to suicide watch shortly after he was convicted and demanding a death sentence a few years ago. On May 23, the jury announced that he could not reach a unanimous decision and sentenced the jury to hang. According to the Huffington Post, a new jury will be elected to determine the fate of Arias. This is scheduled for July 18th. At this point, she may be sentenced to death, life imprisonment or parole within 25 years. The Jodialian case has been reported in many media 24 hours a day, raising new interest in the judicial system.

43 WHO IS ROBERT DURST?

"What the hell did I do? Of course I killed them all."

On Saturday, March 14, 2015, Robert Durst, the son of a New York City real estate tycoon, was arrested in connection with the 2000 Susan Berman murder and the disappearance of his ex-wife Kathleen Durst in 1982. Durst's arrest occurred after a filmmaker in the HBO series The Jinx confessed that Durst confessed to "killing everything" while wearing a live microphone. The Jinx is an HBO miniseries that closely investigates Durst's involvement in the disappearance of his ex-wife and Berman's death.

Robert Durst first became a national topic after it was declared in 1982 that his wife Kathleen was missing. While many speculated that he was involved in his disappearance, Durst remained innocent throughout the search for Kathleen.

Durst became national news again in 2001 when he was discovered to have pretended to be a silent woman in Galveston, Texas during an investigation into the death of a man named Morris Black. Durst apparently fled to Texas after authorities began seeking new leads in his former wife's lawsuit.

He was charged with the murder of Black after Durst was discovered shoplifting in Pennsylvania. Admitting to dismantle Black's body, Durst claimed that Black was accidentally killed when two men grabbed Durst's pistols. Durst's self-defense claims worked and he was acquitted of the murder charges.

The continued presence of Durst in headlines across the country has heightened suspicion of involvement in the 2000 Berman murder. After meeting at graduate school, Durst and Berman became friends and were close until Berman died. At the time of Berman's death, she was to be interrogated by police about Kathleen's disappearance. Many suspected Berman knew of Durst's secret and killed her to bury him.

Robert Durst cannot be retried as Morris Black was murdered in 2001, but attempts to disappear Kathleen and Berman. Jinx's in-depth investigation provided the prosecution with a great deal of new evidence, including Durst's Mike confession. While some are worried that confession may be deemed unacceptable, criminal law scholars say prosecutors need only show that the tape has not been tampered with to allow.

44 SISTER CATHY CESNIK & JOYCE MALECKI

In 2017, Netflix was called and reincarnated in the original documentary liberation keeper in 1969 with the unsolved murder of sisters Kathy Cesnik and Joyce Malecki. Taught the drama that she was a Catholic sister), Catholic High School for all girls in Baltimore.

On November 7, 1969, Cathy Cesnik left her apartment in Catonsville to buy her sister's engagement gift. She never returned, and it was found that her car was illegally parked across her apartment. The car got stuck in mud that was not there the day before. Police searched Cathy Cesnik, but found nothing. Two months later, on January 3, Chesnick's body was discovered by Hunter and his son at an unofficial garbage dump in Landsdown, Maryland. She died of a skull fracture and cerebral hemorrhage.

Joyce Malecki was a 20-year-old office worker at a liquor dealer in Baltimore. On November 11, 1969, Marecki had planned to shop at Halundale Mall in Glen Burnie, Maryland, and then meet his boyfriend in Fort Mead for dinner. The search continued when she didn't show up for dinner. Her body was found two days later on the banks of the Little Patuxent River in Fort Meade. She was tied up, strangled and drowned.

The keeper called attention to a possible relationship between the killings of Chesnic and Marecki and allegations of sexual abuse at Archbishop Keow. Former school students allege that Father Joseph Masquel sexually abused many girls at school while Sister Kathy worked at Keio. One of the girls who confessed to Chesnik felt that Chesnik would take care of her. One ex-student claimed that Masquel took her to see Cassie Chesnick's body and said, "Do you know what happens when you say bad things about people?" The place is her body. It was different from where it was finally discovered, but it was the same as where Marekki's body was discovered. Maskel died in 2001 and is still considered a suspect in the killing of Chesnic.

45 DEVIL'S NIGHT

Devil's Night, the name of the eve of Halloween, refers to the vandalism and arson of abandoned assets before and after Halloween. Devil's Night started many years ago as a gentle mischievous "prank night" of toilet paper houses and games like Ding Dong Groove. However, these mischiefs developed into serious acts of vandalism and arson in the 1970s, and have since continued to occur on the days surrounding Halloween holidays.

Devil's Night is believed to have begun in Detroit and then spread rapidly to other cities along the United States' Last Belt. Due to rising unemployment, foreclosure and economic downturn, many buildings in metropolitan areas have been abandoned and abandoned. These original homes became the target of the vandals, and the three-day and nighttime arson cases surrounding Halloween in the 1970s and 1980s increased exponentially. Detroit arson rates were between 500 and 800 fires in a typical year. These numbers began to decline in the 1990s, due to government initiatives such as curfew and overall increases in community and police behaviour. Neighbors also organized a community watch program, posted signs on the abandoned building, saying "This building is being monitored," in hopes of stopping the vandals.

Although the destructive nature of Devil's Night has diminished in recent years, there is always the fear of a resurgence. The economic downturn, rising unemployment, and thousands of blockades and abandoned buildings in cities like Detroit could revive Devil's Night. In 2010, more than 50,000 residents assisted community patrols, volunteered to protect the neighborhood from Detroit arsonists, and police tracked known arsoners. With community support and police intervention, cities like Detroit will have fun rather than fear Halloween.

46 WHO IS AL CAPONE?

Al Capone was born in Brooklyn, New York in 1899. After graduating from school in sixth grade, he spent two years as a gang member in two gangs: Brooklyn Rippers and Forty Sieves Jr. After working as a guard, he worked for a man named Johnny Torio. Capone accepted when Torrio invited him to join him in Chicago in 1920. The two started working together for the gang of Big Jim Colossimo and took advantage of the ban by distributing illegal liquor.

Korodimo was assassinated and a high-ranking trio was assigned. However, this arrangement did not last long. In 1925, the trio became another victim of an attempted assassination. This weakened Torio asked Capone to become the new boss. Capone was as charismatic as he was and was favored by men who called him "Big Fellow".

With the help of Capone, they managed to expand the industry, and Capone made a legitimate investment and even a dye factory. He built a terrible reputation for himself, and slowly but steadily, he and his gang eliminated their rivals.

On February 14, 1929, the Alcapone gang was part of what is now known as the St. Valentine's Day massacre, resulting in the death of seven men who worked for Capone's rival, Bagsmoran.

On October 17, 1931, Capone was sentenced to 11 years of tax evasion. His sentence began in Atlanta, where he was able to manipulate powers in a cash hiding place. This action brought him a trip to Alcatraz, where he worked for more than four years. He was released in 1939 and died of syphilis in 1947.

47 BONANNO FAMILY

Joseph Bonanno (1905-2002) was a longtime head of one of the top five Italian Italian mafia crime syndicates or "family". From 1931 to 1966, Bonanno ruled the extremely powerful and corrupt Bonanno family and the criminal empire from Brooklyn to California.

The name "Lucky" Luciano is another major figure in Mafia history. In 1931, he, along with the mob boss Vito Genovese, ordered the execution of the crime boss Salvatore Maranzano, on which Bonanno was working, and inadvertently gave Bonanno his opening. Bonanno took over the Maranzano criminal organization. It was then called the Bonanno family. The artwork is also nominated by Stepheno Magadino, a cousin of Bonanno. Bonanno and Magadino were estranged in the mid-1960s when Bonanno tried to build his position as one of the five most powerful bosses. He arranged the assassination of two other top bosses, the Luccase family Thomas Luces and the Gambino family Carlo Gambino (the rest of the mobs were Colombo and Genovese).

Incredibly, Joe Bonanno was convicted of a serious crime in 1980 at the age of 75. Police subsequently imprisoned him for obstructing justice and civil insults in court.

In 1991, Bonanno hinted at his position on the Commission, the American Mafia's agency, through his calligraphic work he created using colored ink and paper. In this artistic artifact, Bonanno describes himself as "being a good father," according to old traditions, to be as right and right as possible. These words of revelation wrote A man in honor of Echo (1983), which he said earlier in his autobiography, he wrote, "I am the father of a family who was like a head of state... I He had to have diplomacy with other families." In the same book, he also formed and reigned "a kind of shadow government that coexisted with the official government" of the "old tradition". I admitted that I was inside a man. Many known Mafia leaders expressed opposition to the book, saying that Bonanno violated their Code of Honor. Bonanno defended the book as an expression of his lifestyle and tradition beyond the law of silence.

Bonanno died spontaneously in 2002 at the age of 97 with friends and family. Bonanno syndicate still exists.

48 THE CRIMES OF BUGSY SIEGEL

Bugsy Siegel was born on 28th February 1906 in Brooklyn, New York. At birth, he was given the name Benjamin by his Jewish immigrant parents. Siegel was brought to crime early on. He grew up in the criminal section of Williamsburg, where there were Irish and Italian gangs. Siegel began his criminal life by forcing money from the New York's Lower East Side tout and launching Meyerlanski and Bagsmeier gang, whom he met at the age of 12. Bagsmeier Gang was in the band Siegel is believed to have hidden his friend Acapone when a warrant was issued to Capone on murder charges.

In the 1920s, Siegel was a prominent player in a new criminal group. This is where Siegel got the nickname Baggie because of his unstable nature. This group of criminals was organized by Charles "Lucky" Luciano and other Italian gangs whose goal was to kill many of New York's veteran gangs. In 1931, Siegel was hired to execute Joe "Boss" Masseria with four others, a Sicilian gangster. The men were executed on April 15 of that year and shot Masseria at Nuova Villa Tammaro on Coney Island. In 1937 Siegel moved to California and took his pirated and gambling racket with him. While there, he set up a gaming field and a maritime gaming boat. Siegel also integrated existing rackets for prostitution, drugs and bookbinding. He lived a luxurious life in Beverly Hills. Siegel had a palace-like property, rubbing his elbows against Hollywood sultans and starlets, and had frequent Hollywood parties. On November

22, 1939, Siegel was one of the gang members who murdered Harry'Big Green' Greenberg after threatening Greenberg to become a police informant. Siegel's criminal partner was Whity Krakower, two unnamed gang members. Siegel was tried in murder in September 1941, and Krakowa was killed before being tried.

In 1945, Siegel moved to Los Angeles with Chicago Mob actress, money runner Virginia Hill, who tended to intimidate Hollywood stars. He has been dating Hill since the late 1930s. Reported to have received $5 million in funding from the Eastern Crime Syndicate, Siegel began implementing his plans to build a gambling mecca in the Nevada Desert. Construction of Flamingo Hotel and Casino quickly exceeded the budget of over $6 million. Much of the waste was discovered to be due to Siegel's mismanagement of money. Siegel was convinced that he could attract thousands of vacationers, so he demanded the best money could buy. Meyerlanski, a prominent member of his former criminal partner, Eastern Syndicate, was never content with Siegel's betrayal.

On the evening of June 20, 1947, a large number of bullets rapidly blasted through the windows of his home's living room, killing him brutally at 42. Later, three Lansky cohorts entered the Flamingo Hotel and declared a takeover. Lanski denied Siegel's involvement in the death, but it is believed that Siegel was killed in a syndicate order beyond undue suspicion.

49 WHO SHOT FRANK COSTELLO?

Francesco Castilia was born on January 26, 1891 in Consenza, Italy. His family moved to East Harlem in New York at the age of four. Francesco eventually became the leader of the 104th Street gang, a Harlem-based Italian gang. He began to carry out small operations such as robbery, assault and robbery, and soon began to make a name for himself as a criminal.

In 1916 he legally changed his name to Frank Costello. Costello was arrested multiple times from 1908 to 1917 when he was released in 1917 when he fell in love with his childhood friend Lauretta Giegerman and eventually married after he got married in 1918. Ciro Terra Nova was a very powerful Spanish Harlem capo, the Morero family.

While working for the Morello gang, Costello met Lucky Luciano and soon made friends with him. They partnered with Meyerlanski, Baggie Siegel, Vito Genovese and Gaeter Norchesse. This alliance will be the starting point for a national criminal organization that started in New York. The group began to get caught up in robbery, extortion, theft, gambling, and drugs, but later during the ban, they focused on pirated editions. Their pirated version of the 1920s was funded by Arnold Rothstein.

Frank Costello got along with many politicians at Tammany Hall and helped criminal groups. These relationships helped the syndicate to buy favor from judges, police, politicians, local lawyers, and city authorities. This domination of local governments immediately began a power struggle between the two members of the syndicate. The Masseria family and the Maranzano family immediately went to war and divided the syndicate. To end the war and continue their business, Costello, Lansky, Luciano, Siegel have decided to kill the heads of both families.

Lucky Luciano was convicted of running a prostitution ring and sentenced to at least 30 years in prison, thus handing his power to Vito Genovese in 1936. Costello was appointed as a replacement for the Luciano family.

After Genovese returned to the United States and acquitted of all accusations, he assumed that he would take on his former role as leader of the Luciano family. When Costello rejected their support, a long process of violence and hatred began.

Most were promulgating the fifth amendment when all Mafioso were called upon to appear before the Grand Jury at the Kefauber hearing, but Costello did not. Costello argued that he had paid taxes and carried out legitimate operations. He left the hearing but was arrested and charged in 1952 for disrespecting the Senate charges.

After serving three years, Costello appealed and was released from prison. Soon Vito Genovese made his move against Costello. Genovese hired Gunman Vincent Gigante to shoot Costello in his head. Miraculously, Costello lived and eventually settled with Genovese. Genovese has allowed Costello to continue his illegal gambling activity in Louisiana and Florida as a peace treaty with him. Costello retired soon, but continued to be involved in the New York Mafia. He quickly won the name "Underworld Prime Minister". In 1973, at the age of 82, Frank Costello died of a heart attack at Manhattan Hospital.

50 GAMBINO CRIME FAMILY

The Gambino Crime Family is one of the most famous criminal organizations in America. The family was born in the early 1900s under the direction of Salvatore Dakira. They became one of the "five families" in New York and joined the "committee" governing committee for organized crime families founded by Charlie "lucky" Luciano.

Salvatore d'Aquila was killed in 1928 and family dominion was transferred to Frank Scully. Although Scales had been in power for only three years, the next crime boss, Vincent Mangano, ruled for 20 years, helping to better establish his family as one of the largest criminal organizations in the world. It was By 1951, Albert Anastasia was best known for taking control and overseeing an organization called Murder Incorporated, which carried out hundreds of mob-related assassinations. Not only was Anastasia considered very dangerous, many of his own people considered him crazy. His crew conspired against him, and he was killed in 1957.

The next head of the family was Carlo Gambino, one of the most successful crime bosses in history. Gambino strengthened their families, significantly raised their profit levels and kept them out of the public eye as much as possible. He avoided any connection to criminal activity and managed his family without spending a day in prison until 1976.

Gambino died in 1976 and placed his family under the control of his brother-in-law Paul Castellano. This angered the second commander of Gambino, Anielo "Neil" Delacross, but Castellano took over peacefully and held Delacross in an authoritative position. Many members of the organization were not happy with the way Castallano ran the family. They thought he acted too much like a business owner and not like Don. Two weeks after Dellacroce's death in 1985, Castellano was killed at the order of his supreme one, John Gotti.

Gotti took over control of the Gambino criminal family with his deputy commander, Salvatore "Samiza Bull" Grabano. For years, Gotty successfully escaped criminal charges and successfully escaped convictions in three separate trials. This made his nickname "Tef London".

In the early 1990s, the situation in Gotti changed. His boss Grabano was arrested and told authorities about Gotis' criminal conduct. Gotti was sentenced to imprisonment and his son John Gotti Jr. became the heir to the family crime business.

51 THE CRIMES OF JACK DIAMOND

Jack Legs Diamond was born on July 10, 1897 in Philadelphia, PA. He came from an Irish family of immigrants. When his mother Sarah died in 1913, he moved to Brooklyn, New York with his father and brother. Diamond began to associate with a local gangster in New York as his father left him unsupervised and starved of food. He was associated with well-known gangsters such as Arnold Rothstein and Jacob Olgen. He was known to commit theft and heinous crimes until 1920.

The era of bans began in the 1920s and became an important opportunity for organized crime. Around this time, Diamond began his career in making profits from alcohol smuggling. He organized a truck robbery to recover his personally owned Speakeasy liquor and immediately advanced to organized crime boss status immediately after ordering the murder of Nathan Kaplan.

Diamond married a woman named Alice Schiffner in 1926. Alice Schiffner was loyal to him even for his famous criminal activity and mistress. Those who knew the diamond, including his wife, described him as very violent and murderous. Diamond was publicly murdered in 1929 by his man in his nightclub, but authorities were unable to hold the charges due to the harassment and killing of a major witness by Diamond and his crew.

Diamond later moved to Accra, New York to rest. So he started a large-scale beer smuggling business. Diamond participated in robbery with the crew and was often shot. He managed to get over the bullet wounds and gave him the nickname "Clay Dove." In 1931, Diamond was arrested for kidnapping and torture by Gordon Parks. On December 18, 1931, Diamond was acquitted and went home to celebrate. He was murdered in his house that night. Many speculate that either a police officer or a rival gang eventually killed Jack Diamond, but a year and a half later his wife was also killed at home.

157